EASY ADULT PIANO
Beginner's Course
An Easy Learning System

Welcome to the EASY ADULT PIANO Learning System, a new, three-part method that will show you how to make music at the piano AND have a lot of fun doing it.

How is it done? . . . By using familiar songs supported by simple examples and exercises, all using Notes-That-Name-Themselves. In no time you'll be capable of playing many of the popular tunes you've always wanted to play.

Part 1 introduces the fundamentals of music and enough keyboard technique to help anyone play songs, using Easy Beginner arrangements.

The second part prepares you to move on to a higher level of playing, using Easy Pro arrangements.

Part 3 is a special supplement containing additional songs for you to enjoy while learning Parts 1 and 2.

BONUS SECTION - Part 3
EASY FAVORITES
Songs to Play and Enjoy

ISBN 0-7935-0242-X

HAL•LEONARD CORPORATION
7777 W. BLUEMOUND RD. P.O. BOX 13819 MILWAUKEE, WI 53213

INTRODUCING THE KEYBOARD

Playing music is probably a lot easier than you think. The following examples will help you get started.

A-B-C Key Stickers are enclosed to help you match the notes on the music with the correct keys on the keyboard. Place them as shown in the illustration. Start with the C key that's beneath the brand-name of the piano (see next page for the location of "MIDDLE C").

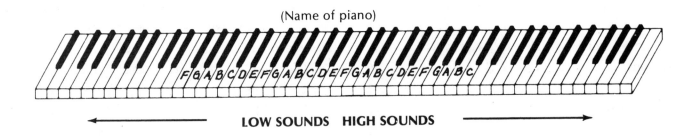

(Name of piano)

F G A B C D E F G A B C D E F G A B C D E F G A B C

⟵ LOW SOUNDS   HIGH SOUNDS ⟶

There are high and low sounds on the piano; high sounds are found to the right, going "up" the keyboard — low sounds are found to the left, going "down" the keyboard. Try this on your piano.

A keyboard is made up of black and white keys. The black keys are in groups of two and three and will help you locate the various white keys.

MIDDLE C

The first step to playing the piano is to locate the key called "MIDDLE C", because it's the main point of reference on your keyboard. Think of it as "home base."

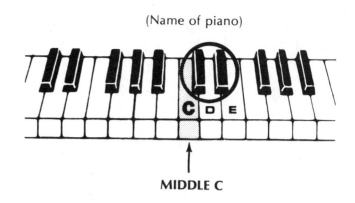

(Name of piano)

MIDDLE C

Start by locating the two-black-key group nearest the middle of your keyboard (usually beneath the brand-name of the piano). The white key just to the left is "MIDDLE C". In our examples on these pages, "MIDDLE C" is shaded gray.

The three-black-key group can be used to locate the white key called "F", just to the left. By knowing where the C and F keys are, you can easily locate the rest of the musical alphabet.

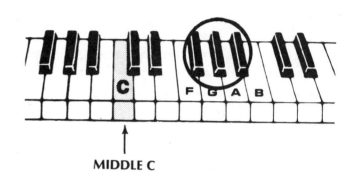

MIDDLE C

MUSICAL ALPHABET

Seven letters — A, B, C, D, E, F, G — make up the musical alphabet. These seven letters repeat over and over to name all the white keys on the piano. Your keyboard guide shows enough of these letters and notes to get you started.

While there is only one key called "MIDDLE C," there are many other C's on the keyboard. Use the two- and three-black-key groups as a guide to locate any letter of the musical alphabet.

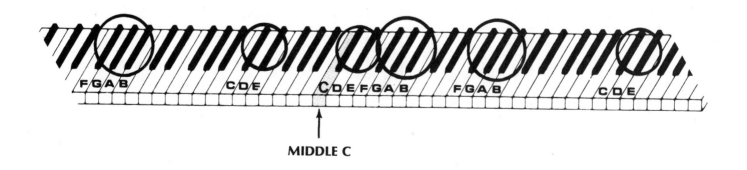

MIDDLE C

THE STAFF

Piano music is written on lines and spaces. A "grand staff" is two staffs, each of five lines and four spaces, joined by a bracket.

(MELODY)

(ACCOMPANIMENT)

The "treble clef" (𝄞) appears at the beginning of the upper staff; the notes that follow are usually played with your hand (Melody). The "bass clef" (𝄢) appears at the beginning of the lower staff; the notes that follow are usually played with your left hand (Accompaniment).

Many people ask why the lines and spaces in the bass and treble staffs are named differently. At one time, music was written on an eleven-line staff but this made notes difficult to read.

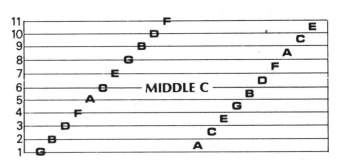

To solve this problem the lines were separated — five on top (𝄞), five on the bottom (𝄢) and the left-over line served as the dividing point, hence the name "Middle C." Coincidentally, on the piano this is the C-key closest to the middle of the keyboard.

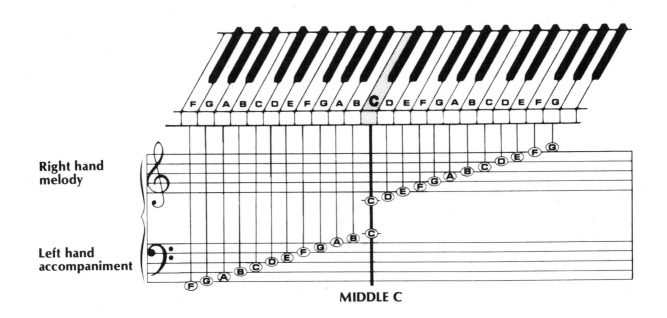

Right hand melody

Left hand accompaniment

MIDDLE C

WHEN THE SAINTS GO MARCHING IN

PLAYING A MELODY

With your right hand, play the first five keys, C-D-E-F-G, one-at-a-time, starting with your thumb on "MIDDLE C."

The illustrations on this page show finger numbers, with each hand numbered 1 through 5, starting with the thumb. Not only are suggested fingerings helpful in this beginning stage; they'll also aid you later on as the music becomes more involved. For now, at least, it's recommended that you observe all suggested fingerings.

Do the same with your left hand, starting at the next C-key to the left of "MIDDLE C."

Now, repeat. This time, leave out the "D" key. Start with one hand — then the other.

Sound familiar? You've just played the first part of WHEN THE SAINTS GO MARCHING IN!

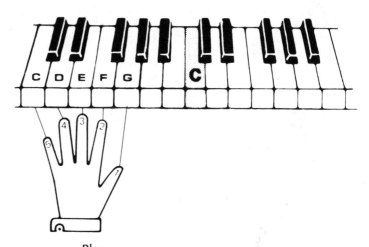

Play . . .
RIGHT HAND: **C** D E F G
FINGERS: 1 2 3 4 5

Play . . .
LEFT HAND: C D E F G
FINGERS: 5 4 3 2 1

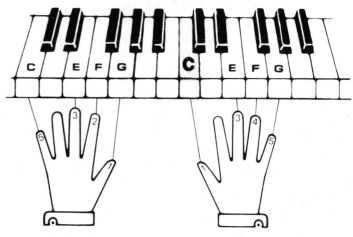

Play . . .
LEFT HAND: C E F G   RIGHT HAND: **C** E F G
FINGERS: 5 3 2 1   FINGERS: 1 3 4 5

WHEN THE SAINTS GO MARCHING IN

Match the letters in the notes on the staff to the
letters on your keyboard guide — and play! All
"MIDDLE C" notes are in brackets.

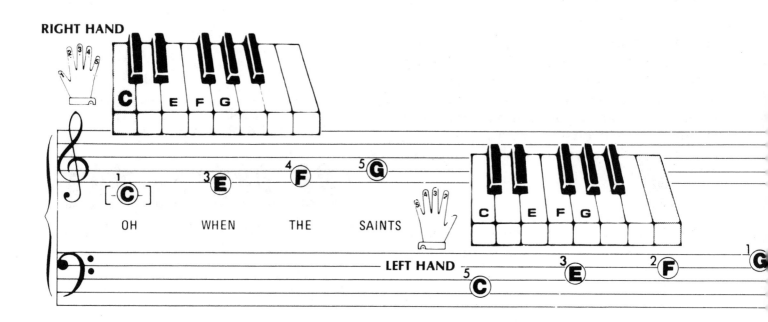

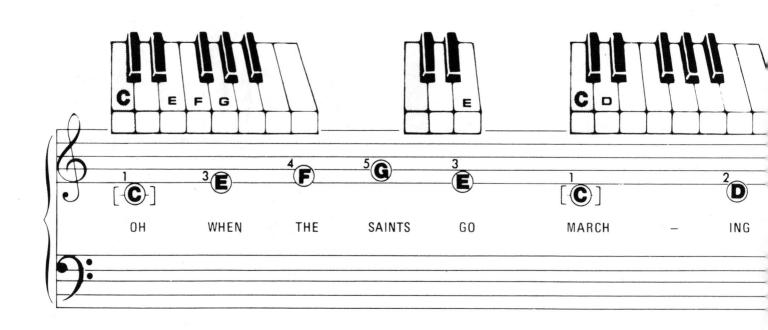

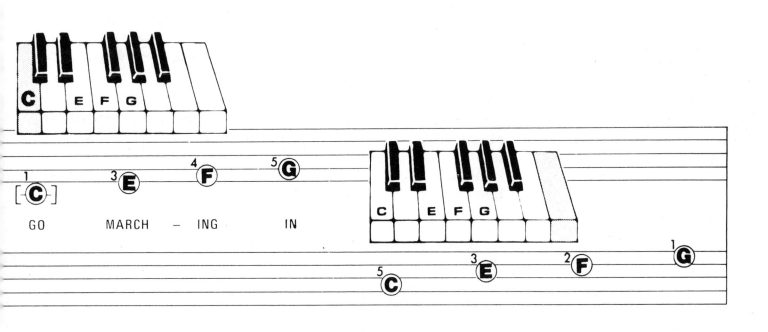

GO   MARCH – ING   IN

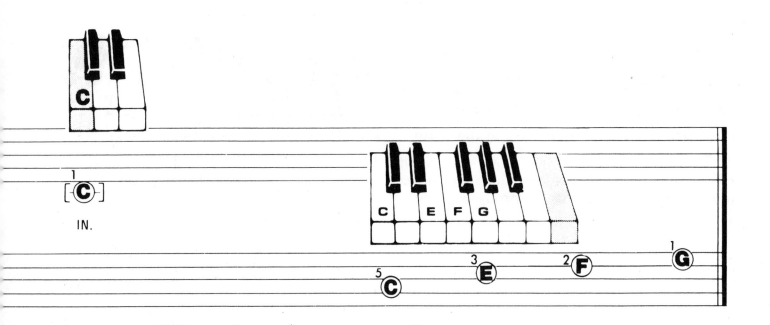

IN.

CHOPSTICKS

BEATS AND HOW TO COUNT THEM

Time, in music, is measured in "beats." To help you understand what beats are, tap your foot in a steady, even manner. Each complete down and up motion equals one beat. To keep track of the beats, a number is counted each time your foot taps the floor.

CHOPSTICKS consists entirely of QUARTER NOTES, each of which is worth ONE BEAT.

Beats grouped together make up certain rhythms. A waltz is a rhythm where beats occur in groups of three; how many times have you heard the phrase "Oom-Pah-Pah"? CHOPSTICKS is a waltz. To help show beats in

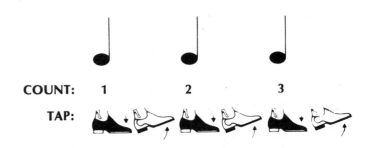

groups of three, "bar lines" are used to divide the staff into "measures." A waltz has three beats in each measure, as shown by the "3" in the example.

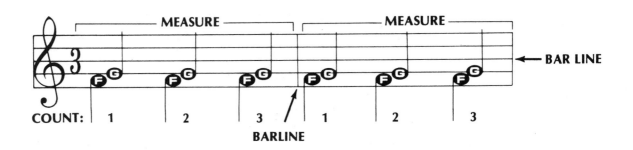

For ease of reading this song, all notes appear in the treble staff. Notes with stems up ♩ are played with your right hand. Notes with stems down ♩ are played with your left hand.

Play each pair of quarter notes **at the same time.**

Here's your starting hand position. Use the index fingers of both hands throughout the song.

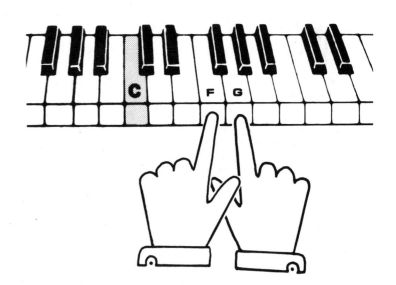

For your convenience, the measures in each song are numbered; reference numbers appear in circles to the left of each line of music.

CHOPSTICKS

COCKLES AND MUSSELS

RHYTHM — BEATS — TIME

Rhythm plays a large part in everyday living; every step you take — each intake of breath — even the cycle of waking and sleeping — is rhythmic.

Music is rhythmic, too, and uses symbols as a visual aid. You already know one—the quarter note (♩). Here are two more . . .

HALF NOTE

2 BEATS

COUNT: 1   2
TAP:

DOTTED HALF NOTE

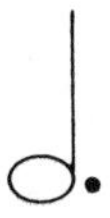

3 BEATS

COUNT: 1   2   3
TAP:

These notes are held for the total number of foot-taps (beats).

TIME SIGNATURE—

"Time signatures" are used to structure beats into uniform measures. $\frac{3}{4}$ is one kind of time signature — the upper number (in this case, 3) always tells how many beats occur in each measure. The lower number, 4, tells you the quarter note receives one beat. You'll learn about other kinds of signatures later on.

COCKLES AND MUSSELS
(Also known as "Sweet Molly Malone")

The keyboards shown here will aid your left hand. The gray MIDDLE C key is indicated.

ROW, ROW, ROW YOUR BOAT

PLAYING CHORD ACCOMPANIMENT

Up to now you've played one note with each hand; this song introduces chords, which provide a background for melodies. A "chord" is a combination of three or more keys played at the same time, mostly by your left hand and mostly in the keyboard area to the left of MIDDLE C.

This song uses only the C chord. The illustration shows how it looks on your music and where to play it on your keyboard. Try it a few times.

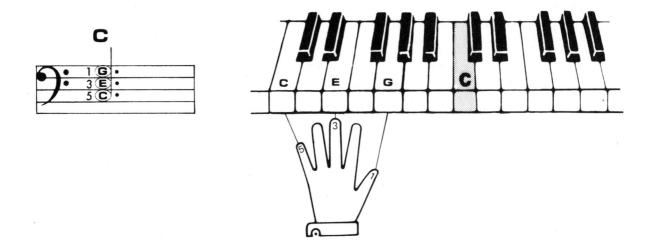

Today's popular sheet music and books also show "chord symbols" above the melody. This letter is a form of "short-hand" that indicates the name of the accompaniment chord written in the bass staff. Most musicians look at just chord symbols and, from experience, know which notes to play — they don't even look at the bass staff. As you become more proficient at playing chords, you may also want to do the same. Do whatever is easiest for you. (You'll find more information on playing chord accompaniment on page 19.)

TIES

A "tie is a curved line placed between two or more notes. Ties are used to make longer-sounding tones. The example shown would be played as one note, six beats long. Letters don't appear in notes following ties.

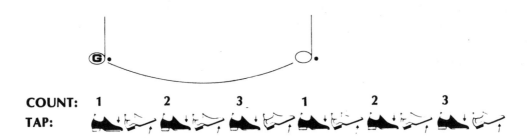

COUNT: 1   2   3   1   2   3
TAP:

Chords may also be tied. Hold each chord until the next chord symbol appears above the music.

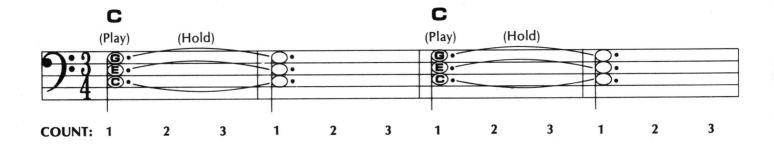

COUNT: 1   2   3   1   2   3   1   2   3   1   2   3

NOTE: In measures 5 and 6 of the song, your right thumb must cross under your second finger to play the E note.

ROW, ROW, ROW YOUR BOAT

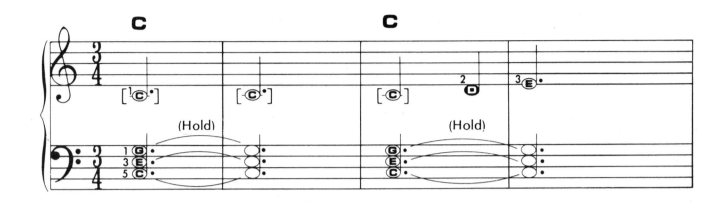

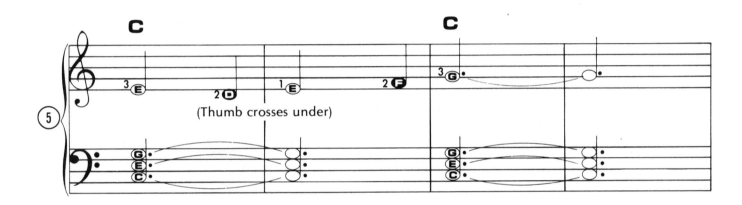

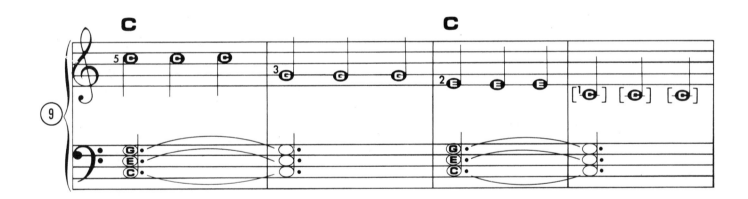

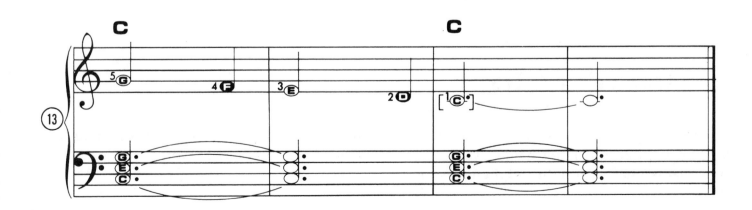

A. MATCHING

Match the numbers in the left hand column to the correct answers in the right hand column.

1.

2. 𝅗𝅥

3. A B C D E F G

4. 𝄢

5.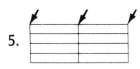

6. 𝄞

7. 𝅗𝅥.

8. ♩

9. **C**

10.

11. (chord)

(**8**)   Quarter note

(   )   Bass clef

(   )   Staff

(   )   Tie

(   )   Treble clef

(   )   Bar lines

(   )   Chord

(   )   Dotted half note

(   )   Musical alphabet

(   )   Half note

(   )   Chord symbol

B. NAME THE NOTES

On the next page is the melody of SKATERS WALTZ, without the letter-names. Write the letter-name near each note and then play the melody. HINT: One note is included that you haven't played before. Watch the ties!

SKATERS WALTZ

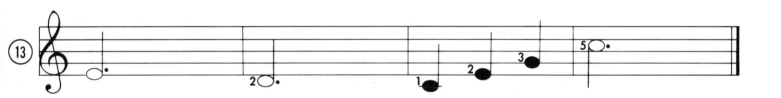

NOTE: A complete arrangement of SKATERS WALTZ appears in the "Easy Favorites" section of this book (see next page for more information).

ANSWERS TO REVIEW

⑬ E D C E G C
⑨ D C G F E
⑤ F A B B
B. SKATERS WALTZ: E G A A
A. Matching: (8) (4) (1) (10) (6) (5) (11) (7) (3) (2) (9)

OTHER SONGS YOU CAN NOW PLAY . . .

The "Easy Favorites" section contains more music you can play as you work your way through this book. Because there are two arrangements of each song—an **Easy Beginner** and an **Easy Pro**—you can start right now. With what you've learned up to now, you can play the arrangements shown here by reading the notes appearing for both hands.

THEME "FROM THE NEW WORLD" SYMPHONY
EASY BEGINNER

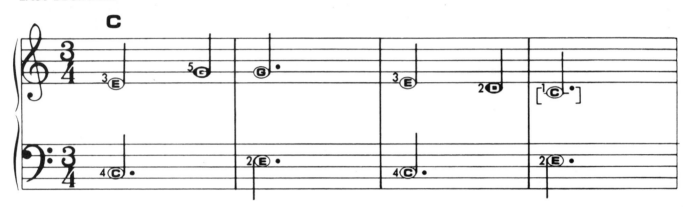

BEAUTIFUL BROWN EYES
EASY BEGINNER

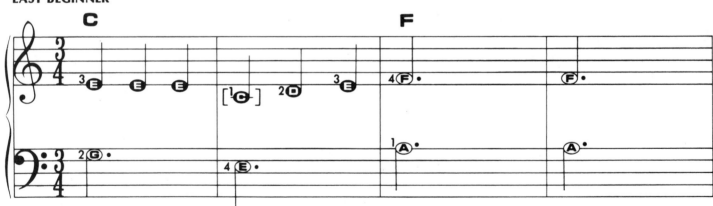

At various places in this book, other songs in "Easy Favorites" are also listed for your playing enjoyment.

HOME SWEET HOME

PICK-UP NOTES

"Pick-up notes" are any notes before the first complete measure of a song. The example below has a $\frac{3}{4}$ time signature, but the first measure has only two beats; the third beat appears at the end of the song. Incidentally, Measure no. 1 is the first complete measure after the pick-up notes.

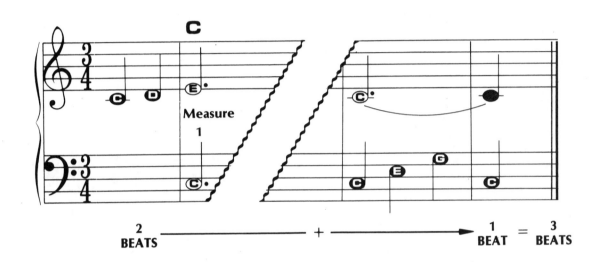

PLAYING CHORD ACCOMPANIMENT

As you learned on page 13, a "chord" is a combination of three or more keys played at the same time. You also learned that the C chord is made up of the notes C-E-G. This is called the ROOT POSITION of the chord because the C note is the lowest note.

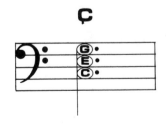

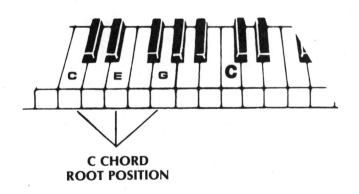

**C CHORD
ROOT POSITION**

All chords can be played in different positions on the keyboard. For example, the next illustration shows the 1ST INVERSION of the C chord. It's called an "inversion" because the C note has been moved to the top of the chord (inverted).

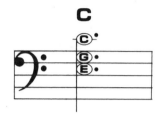

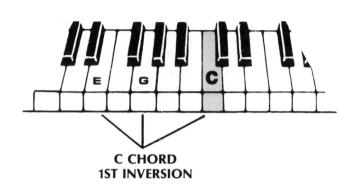

C CHORD
1ST INVERSION

Moving the bottom E note to the top, creates the 2ND INVERSION of the C chord.

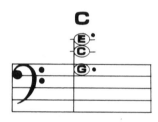

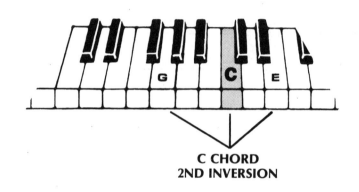

C CHORD
2ND INVERSION

Notice that each position still has the same three note letter names — they're just in a different order.

If you again invert the bottom note of the 2ND INVERSION, you create the ROOT POSITION (C-E-G) but in a different location on the keyboard.

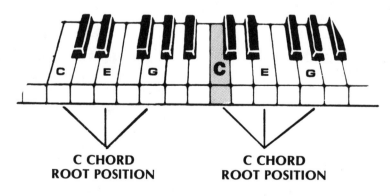

C CHORD   **C CHORD**
ROOT POSITION   **ROOT POSITION**

In most cases, the higher ROOT POSITION would not be used for an accompaniment chord because melody notes may "bump into" the chord notes.

20

Each inversion can also be played in a different location on the keyboard. Use the location that doesn't bump into melody notes.

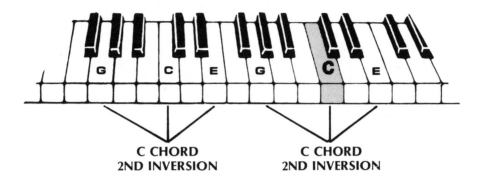

The next song HOME SWEET HOME uses two additional chords, the F chord and the G chord. The example shows the different positions of each. (Only one location is shown for the 2ND INVERSIONS because the higher ones would be too high.)

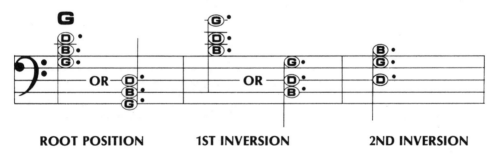

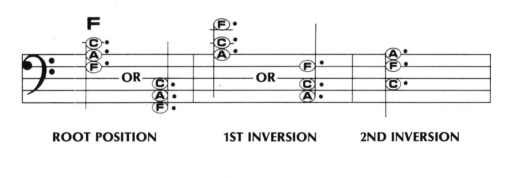

From this point on, chord symbols are shown on all songs should you want to play a chord accompaniment. A chord chart is also provided on page 38 showing chords (and their inversions) to assist you.

OTHER SONGS YOU CAN NOW PLAY . . .

Try the Easy Beginner arrangements of MARIANNE, MICHAEL ROW THE BOAT ASHORE, and LONG, LONG AGO in the "Easy Favorites" section

HOME SWEET HOME

WHEN THE SAINTS GO MARCHING IN

TIME SIGNATURE —

$\frac{4}{4}$ is another kind of time signature. The upper number, 4, tells you there are four beats in each measure; the lower 4 tells you the quarter note receives one beat.

WHOLE NOTE

○

4 BEATS

COUNT: 1   2   3   4

TAP:

THE PEDALS ON YOUR PIANO

At the lower front of your piano, you'll see one, two, or three pedals, depending on the piano model you own.

SOFT PEDAL or UNA CORDA

SOSTENUTO, BASS DAMPER or PRACTICE PEDAL

SUSTAIN or DAMPER PEDAL

The pedal farthest to the left (whether there are two or three) is used for playing softly. The middle pedal name and usage varies from one piano model to another; it's not used at all in the EASY ADULT PIANO Learning System so you needn't concern yourself with it.

The one pedal present on all pianos is called the Sustain or Damper Pedal and that's the one you'll use when you play this song.

When you play a key or chord, and at the same time press down this pedal, the musical tone continues to sustain, or linger, long after your fingers have left the keys. When you release the pedal, the sound stops. This can help you create a really big, full sound if you use the pedal properly.

The example shown is from the ending of WHEN THE SAINTS GO MARCHING IN. Play it without the sustain pedal and then press the pedal and play the example again. You'll really like what you hear!

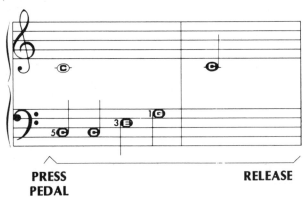

PRESS PEDAL   **RELEASE**

WHEN THE SAINTS GO MARCHING IN

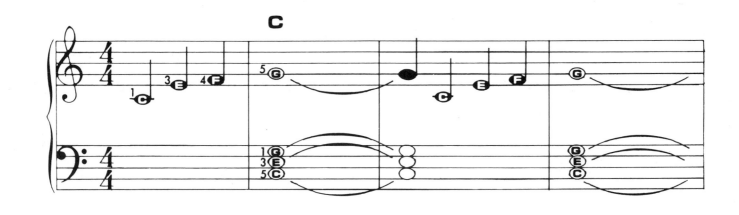

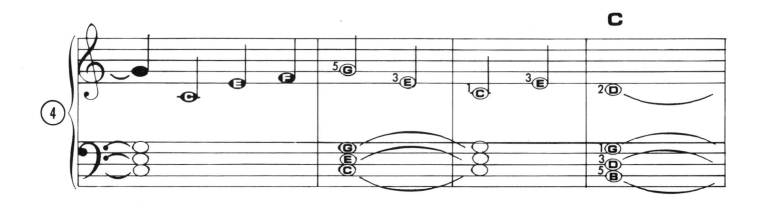

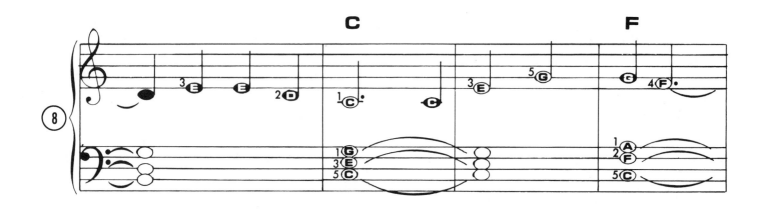

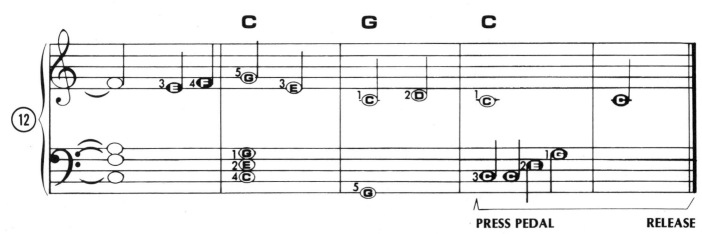

PRESS PEDAL　　　　　　　　　**RELEASE**

MAORI FAREWELL SONG

BROKEN CHORDS

In the last song, you played the notes of the C chord one-at-a-time to create an interesting ending for the arrangement. This same idea can be applied to the accompaniment to add interest and variety to various places within a song. Here's how it works with the C chord . . .

Play each note of the chord separately, starting with the lowest note (Beat 1), then the middle note (Beat 2), the highest note (Beat 3), and the middle note again (Beat 4). Try it.

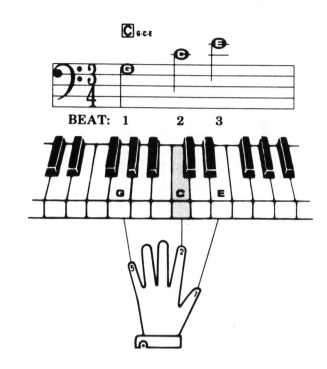

SHARP ♯

This tic-tac-toe symbol, called a "sharp" appears before a note to indicate a raise in pitch (the sound of the note).

To locate D♯, first find D on the keyboard; D-sharp (D♯) is the very next key to the right. It's a black key.

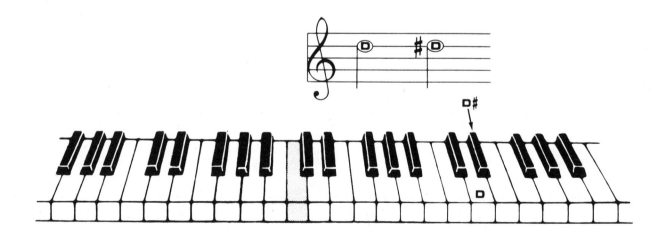

Any sharp key is the very next key to the right, whether that key is black or white.

MAORI FAREWELL SONG
(Popular version known as "Now Is The Hour")

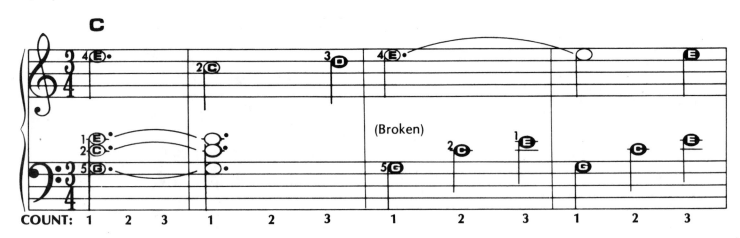

COUNT: 1   2   3   1   2   3   1   2   3   1   2   3

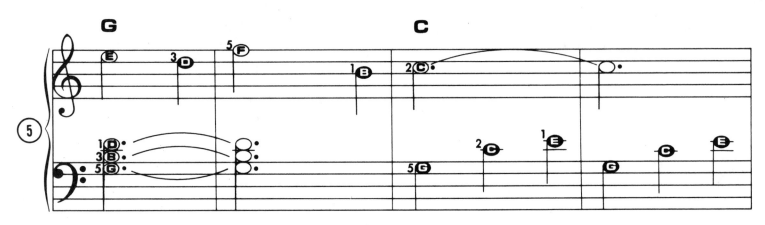

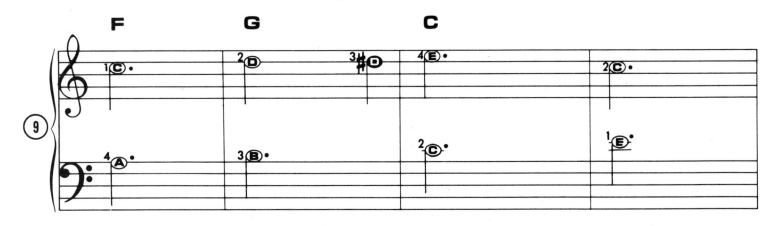

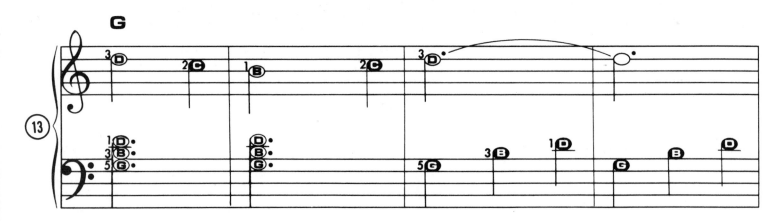

EIGHTH NOTES

Another type of note you should learn to play is the **eighth note**. An eighth note looks a lot like a quarter note, except that it has a flag attached to its stem.

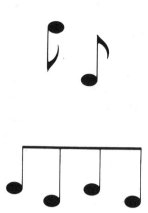

Groups of two or more eighth notes are connected by a bar:

HOW TO COUNT THEM

You already know that quarter notes get one beat, so the logical question seems to be, "How do I count eighth notes?" To answer this, we'll compare counting beats to tapping your foot in time to music.

When you tap beats in an even and steady manner, your foot makes two motions — up and down. Therefore, each beat has two parts,

or halves — an upbeat and a downbeat. The illustration shows this, along with a slightly different way of counting — each down beat gets a number and each upbeat gets the word "and" (&). Start by slowly tapping your foot and counting aloud. Then, try it again, playing the four quarter notes — you'll quickly see how this works.

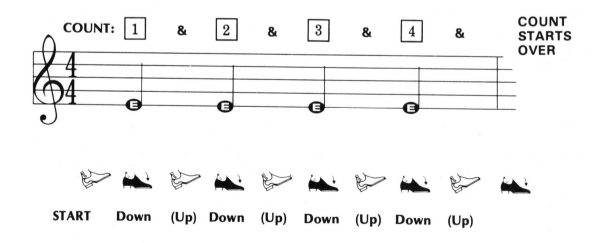

This is the same as the previous example with some eighth notes added. Count and play it a few times.

JINGLE BELLS

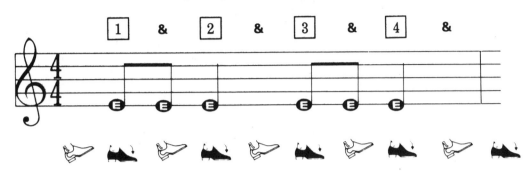

We can now say that an eighth note is one half-beat long. Therefore, two eighth notes are equal to one quarter note.

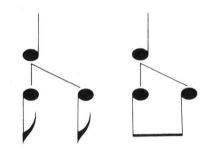

FRERE JACQUES
(Also known as "Are You Sleeping?")

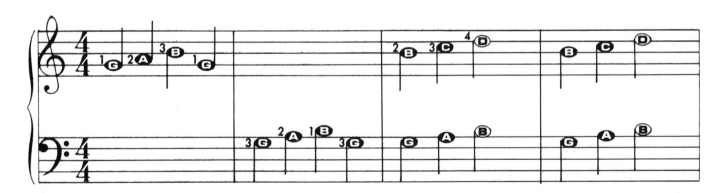

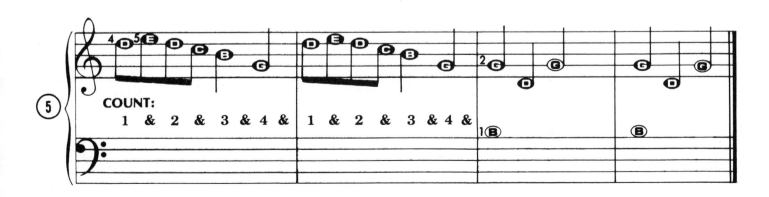

LAVENDER'S BLUE

(Also try the different Easy Beginner arrangement on page 110.)

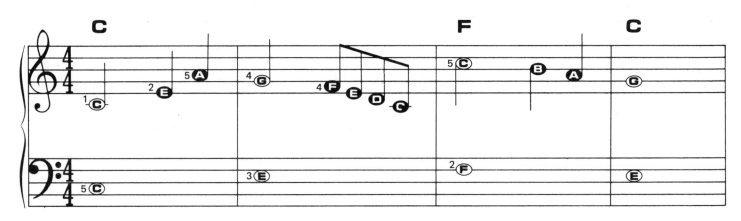

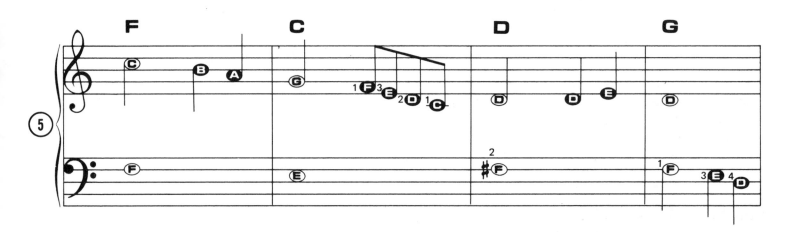

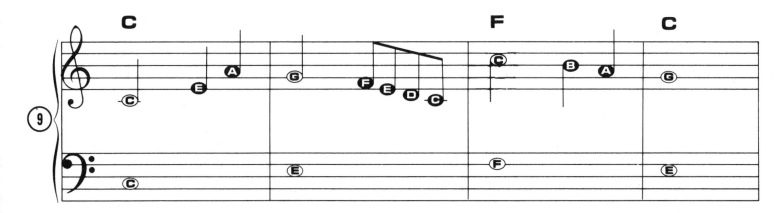

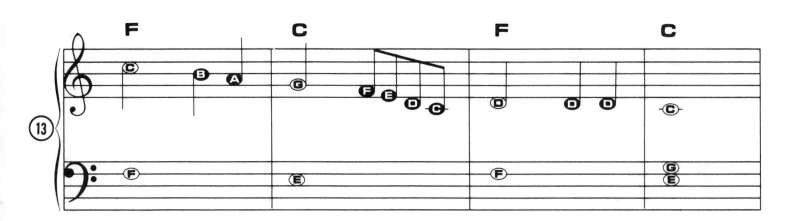

30

GREENSLEEVES

FLAT ♭

This "♭" symbol, called a "flat" appears before a note to indicate a lowering of the pitch (the sound of the note).

To find B♭, first locate B on the keyboard. B-flat (B♭) is the very next key to the left. It's a black key.

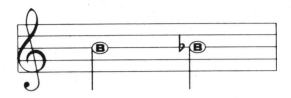

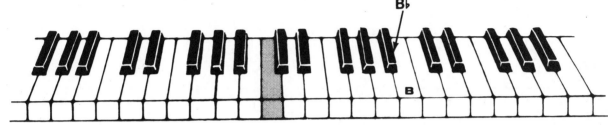

Any flat key is the very next one to the left, whether that key is black or white.

C-sharp (C♯) notes appear in each staff and the D-minor and A chords occur for the first time; locate these before you play the song.

ARPEGGIO

This exciting and professional sound occurs when the notes of a chord are played one-at-a-time, as your hands move up the keyboard.

This style should be used only where two melody notes are tied together for a long time, or to add another type of dramatic ending. Be sure to hold down the sustain pedal when you play an arpeggio.

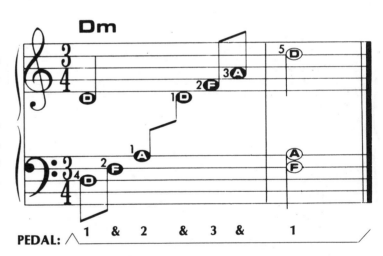

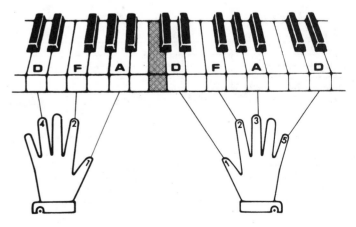

GREENSLEEVES

SUSTAIN
PEDAL

33

RESTS

"Rests" represent silence in music — they tell you when NOT to play. Rests have values just as notes do. Certain rests correspond to certain notes.

EIGHTH REST	QUARTER REST	HALF REST	WHOLE REST
♪	𝄾	▬	▬
1/2 BEAT OF SILENCE	1 BEAT OF SILENCE	2 BEATS OF SILENCE	4 BEATS OF SILENCE or entire measure
EIGHTH NOTE	QUARTER NOTE	HALF NOTE	WHOLE NOTE
♪	♩	♩	○
1/2 BEAT	1 BEAT	2 BEATS	4 BEATS

NATURAL SIGN ♮

To cancel a sharp or flat, a "natural" sign is placed in front of a note.

Practice the melody and accompaniment separately before playing them together.

Notice that most of the sharp, flat and natural signs, called "accidentals," appear in the bass staff.

OCTAVE SIGN *8va*

When this sign is placed above a group of notes, it tells you to play those notes "an octave (8 notes) higher than they're written." In other words, move to the right on your keyboard to the next key having the same letter-name. This occurs a lot in standard music and allows you to play notes outside the staff without your having to figure out their names.

Except for the last three notes, the melody on the entire second page is to be played on octave higher than it's written; the accompaniment, however, does not change.

8va   (Notes written here . . .

. . . are played here)

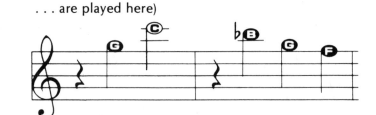

LOCO

At the end of the song, you'll see the word *loco,* an Italian word meaning "place." This cancels the *8va* sign and indicates that, from that point on, the melody notes are to be played "as written."

THEME FROM RACHMANINOFF'S PIANO CONCERTO NO.2

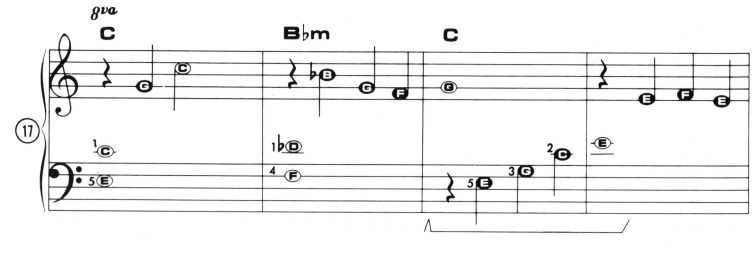

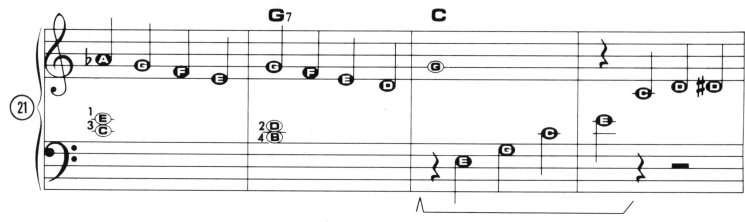

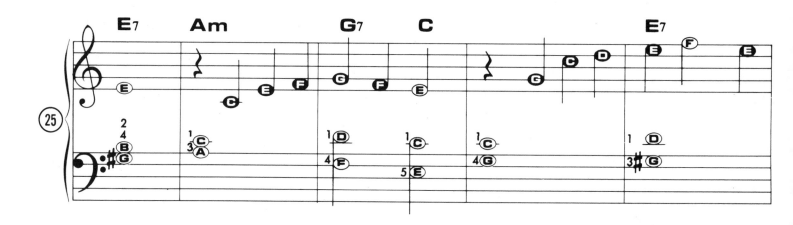

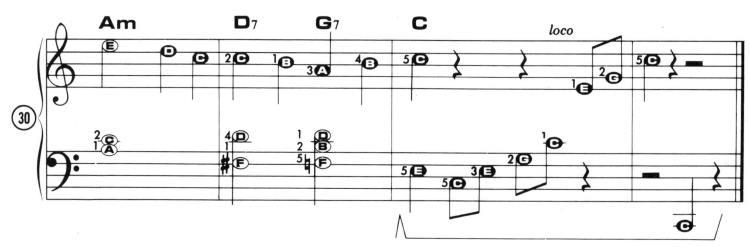

QUIZ

CIRCLE THE CORRECT ANSWER.

1. What kind of note receives 4 beats?
   A. half note
   B. quarter note
   C. whole note

2. The two large numbers at the beginning make up the
   A. lines and spaces
   B. time signature.
   C. fingering.

3. Measures are formed by drawing
   A. bar lines.
   B. clef signs
   C. chord symbols.

4. How many beats are there in each measure of a song having a $\frac{3}{4}$ time signature?
   A. 4 beats
   B. 3 beats
   C. 7 beats

5. How many beats does a half note receive?
   A. 1/2 beat
   B. 1 beat
   C. 2 beats

6. Which one is an eighth note?
   A. ♪
   B. ♩
   C. ○

7. What's the symbol for a sharp?
   A. ♪
   B. $\frac{4}{4}$
   C. ♯

8. What sign means "eight notes higher than written"?
   A. *8va*
   B. ♮
   C. ▬

9. This is a symbol for a whole note
   A. ♩
   B. ○
   C. ♫

10. The symbol for a quarter rest is
    A. ▬
    B. ⅞
    C. ♪

37

CHORD CHART
CHORDS USED IN PART 1

(C, F and G chords are on page 21)

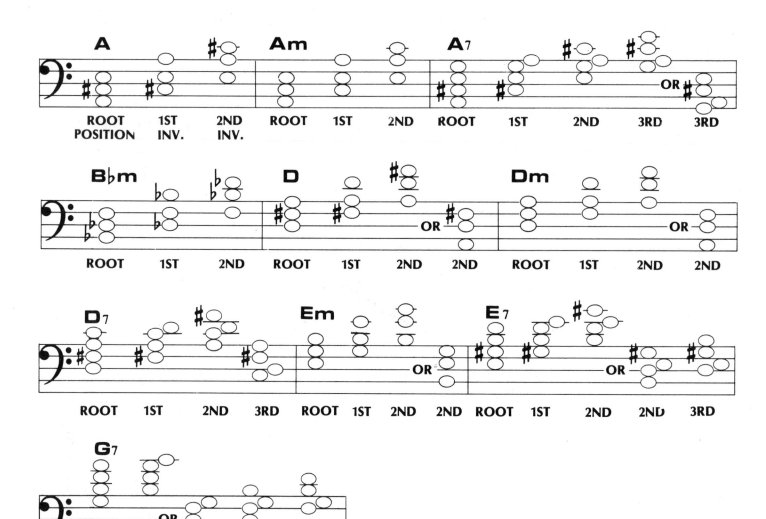

CHORD SYMBOLS

"Chord Symbols" name the chord and the notes used. Since chord symbols are a form of abbreviation, or shorthand, you should be aware of what the different components mean.

M = major (Capital M never appears next to the chord letter — it is understood to be a major chord)
7 = seventh
m = minor

6 = sixth
9 = ninth
+ = augmented
o = diminished

Sometimes these elements are combined:

m6 = minor sixth
M7 = major seventh

CONGRATULATIONS . . .

You've just completed Part 1 of this course and look at what you've learned! In addition, you've been able to entertain yourself and others with some great songs that are enjoyable and easy to play.

Part 2 of the EASY ADULT PIANO Easy Learning System will prepare you for the **EASY PRO** arrangements. These are a definite step-up from **Easy Beginner,** being more pianistic and professional-sounding, yet still easy to play.

Before you begin Part 2, you may want to look over the following material.

REVIEW OF PART 1

STAFF AND NOTES

All piano music is written on a "grand staff" which consists of a "treble staff" and a "bass staff" connected by a bracket.

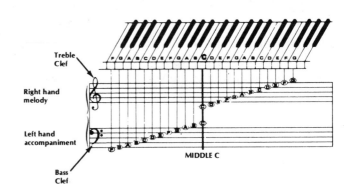

MEASURES AND BAR LINES

The staff is divided into sections by using vertical lines called "bar lines." The sections between the bar lines are called "measures."

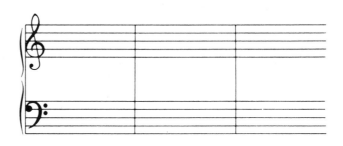

TIME VALUES

In music, time is measured in "beats." The illustration shows the types of notes you'll play and how many beats each type gets.

Rests are shown in the lower part of the illustration, along with the number of beats each type gets. A "rest" indicates a period of silence, when you don't play; they still must be counted, however.

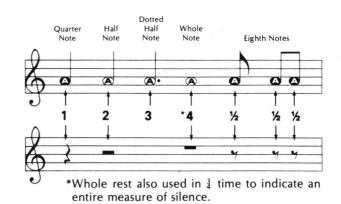

*Whole rest also used in ¾ time to indicate an entire measure of silence.

40

TIME SIGNATURE

The two numbers at the beginning of a song are known as the "time signature." The top number indicates the number of beats in each measure. The bottom number 4 tells you each quarter note (♩) recieves one beat.

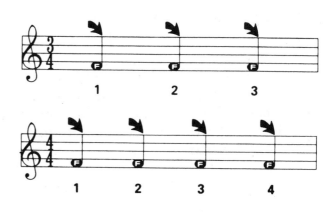

TIES

A "tie" connects notes on the same line of in the same space. It tells you the first note is struck and then held for the total time value of the tied notes.

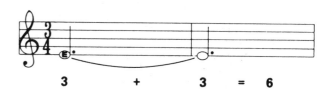

PLAYING THE BLACK KEYS

Sharps and flats tell you when to play the black keys. A "sharp" (♯) tells you to play the very next black key to the right and a "flat" (♭) tells you to play the very next black key to the left. "Natural" signs (♮) are used to cancel sharps and flats.

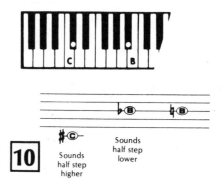

FINGERING

Small numbers appear near some of the notes; these are finger numbers and they'll help you play more smoothly. Think of your fingers as being numbered as shown. They play the keys with the fingers that correspond to the numbers near the notes.

OCTAVE SIGN

This sign tells you to play "an octave higher." In other words, move to the right on your keyboard to the next key having the same letter-name.

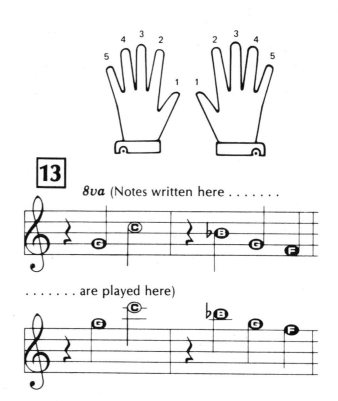

PICK-UP NOTES

"Pick-up notes" are any notes played before the first chord of a song is played. The example below has a $\frac{3}{4}$ time signature, but the first measure has only two beats; the third beat appears at the end of the song.

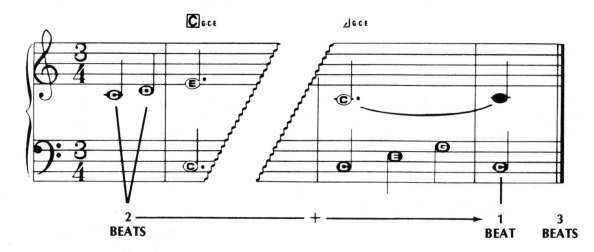

THE SUSTAIN PEDAL

Regardless of how many pedals your piano has, the one pedal present on ALL pianos is called the Sustain, or Loud Pedal.

When you play a key and at the same time press down this pedal, the musical tone continues to sustain, or linger, long after your fingers have left the keys. This can help you create a really big, full sound if you use the pedal properly.

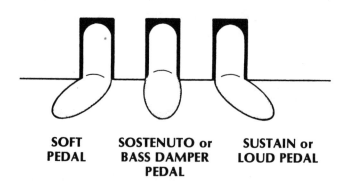

NAME THE KEYS

Name the circled keys. Check your answers when you're finished.

Do this until you can name the keys correctly.

1.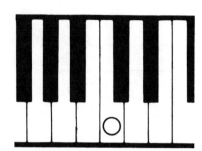

2.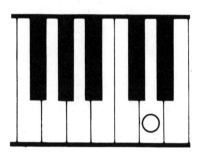

3.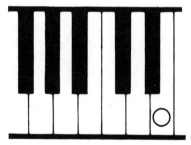

4.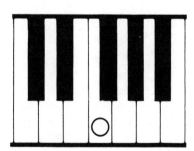

5.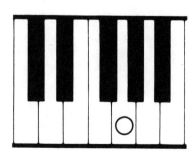

6.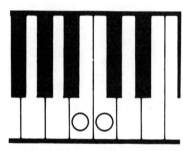

7.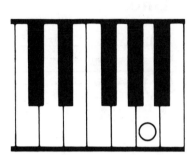

8.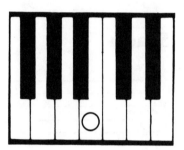

9.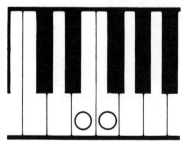

Write the names of the lines and spaces in the illustrations below.

Helpful Hint: Use middle C as a reference point. Notice, as notes skip from line to line, or space to space, you skip a letter.

Lines

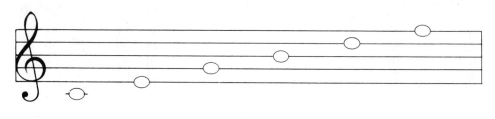

Spaces

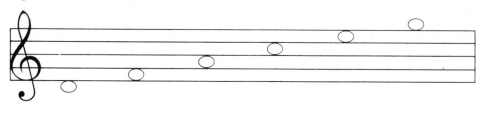

As practice in reading notes, write the names of notes in the exercise below.

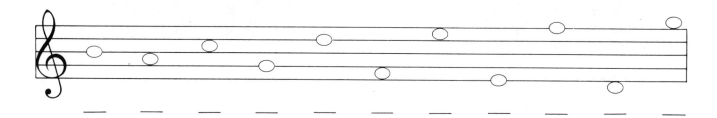

44

LEGER LINES
Also "Ledger"

You've already seen notes written on small lines which are placed above or below the staff. These lines are called leger lines and are an extension of the staff. Though leger lines are not as long as the regular lines of the staff, they do represent specific keys on the keyboard. Notes written on leger lines are shown.

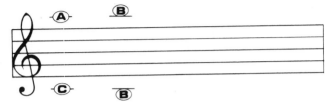

Write in the names of the notes appearing on leger lines in the next illustration.

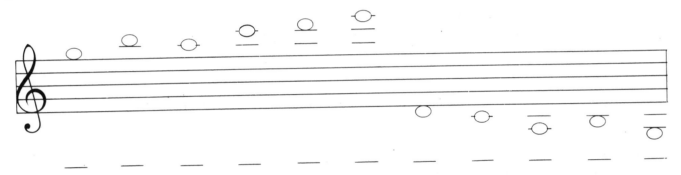

Answers: G B A C D E D C A B C

In the examples below, draw a line from the notes to the correct key. Middle C is indicated in gray to help you.

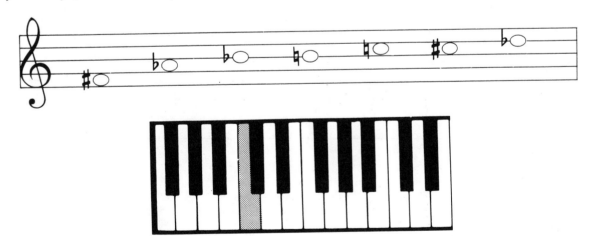

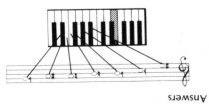

Answers

45

NOTES:

DU, DU LIEGST MIR IM HERZEN

SCALES

A "scale" is a series of eight notes which begin on a given line or space of the staff and end on the next line or space with the same letter-name. Each of the notes is a specific distance from the others in the series; this distance is measured in whole-steps and half-steps. Although there are several kinds of scales, the most common is the "major scale." The starting note of the scale determines the letter-name of the scale (the C scale starts on the C note, etc.) The C, F, and G major scales are shown — notice the pattern of whole-steps (w) and half-steps (1/2) is the same in each case.

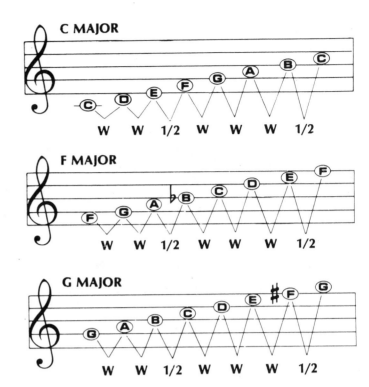

KEY SIGNATURES

In many songs, you'll see one or more sharps or flats printed at the beginning of the music, after the clef sign; this is called the "key signature."

The word "key," means the key-note, or principal note, around which the other tones of a particular song are organized. "Key" also refers to the scale upon which the song is based. The first note of the scale is the same as the key-note of the song.

Any note whose sharp or flat appears in the key signature is to be played sharp or flat throughout the entire song.

A song having no sharps or flats in its key signature is based on the C major scale and is said to be "written in the key of C major."

DOUBLE NOTES

This is the first song in which you'll play double notes with your right hand; along with the melody note, you'll also play a harmony note. Double notes occur starting at measures 17 and

25. Fingering is suggested to help you; be sure to practice these passages separately before you play the entire arrangement.

DU, DU LIEGST MIR IM HERZEN

Medium Fast
Key of G

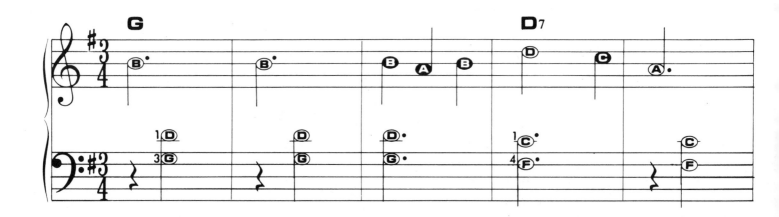

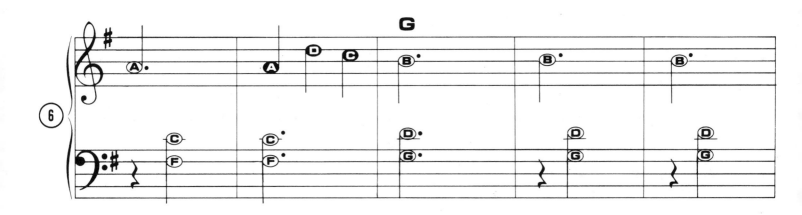

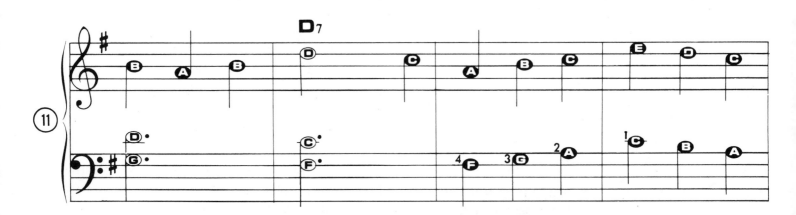

D.S. AL ✛ CODA

You'll notice some new symbols in this song because the song has a "coda." Coda is an Italian word that refers to a short section of music used to end a song.

At measure 16 you'll see the phrase "D.S. al ✛ CODA" this tells you to go back to this sign (𝄋) and replay the measures until you reach this sign (✛); then skip to the coda. Here's how it works:

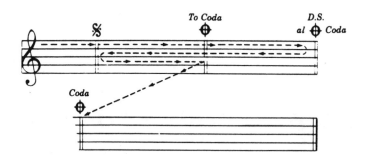

FERMATA 𝄐

The "Fermata" sign indicates a pause, or a hold. Fermata signs appear at the very end of VIENNA LIFE and tell you to hold the notes longer than the indicated time value.

VIENNA LIFE

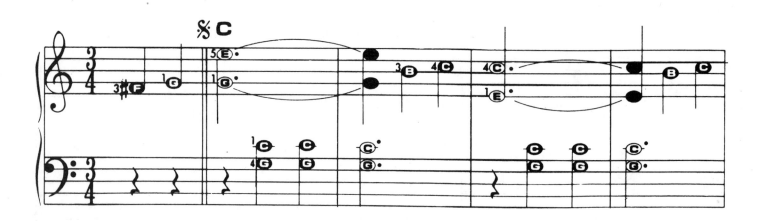

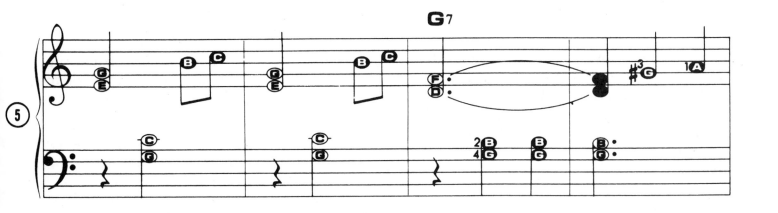

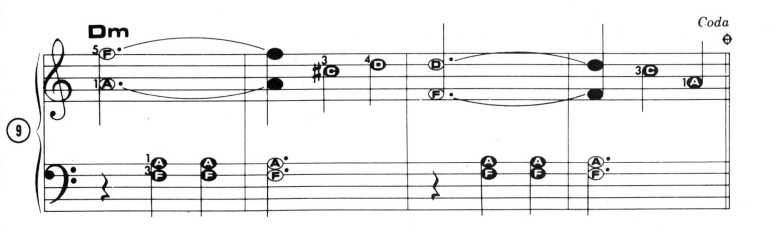

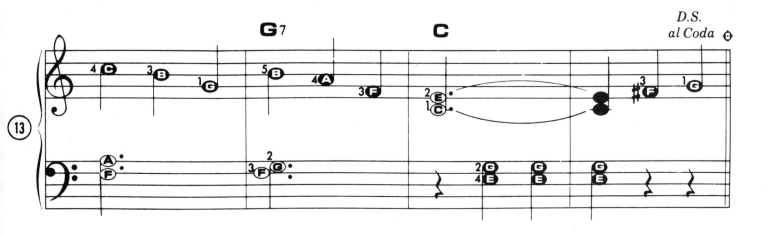

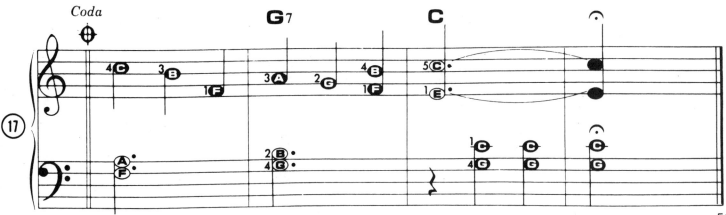

So far, you've played songs with notes-that-name-themselves. BILL BAILEY is the first song you'll play that has no letters in the melody. This helps prepare you for the Easy Pro arrangements found in the EASY FAVORITES SECTION, which also have no letters in the melody. All songs from here on have no letters in the treble staff.

This should be easy for you since you've played so many songs with letters in the notes; you've already learned most of them by association. In addition, many people can already read notes on the treble staff because of playing experience on other instruments (clarinet, violin, etc.). The example shown here reminds you that the letter-names of the spaces spell the word FACE and the letter-names of the lines are an abbreviation for Every Good Boy Does Fine.

You also have your A-B-C Key Stickers to help you. Just match the notes to those shown on the keys. Playing through the melody a couple of times will help you become more familiar with the names of the notes. Then add the accompaniment.

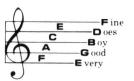

INTRODUCTIONS

Introductions are used in music to "set up" or "get into" the mood of a song. Sometimes introductions, usually four to eight measures long, use parts of the melody or an important rhythm that appears in the song itself. The introduction in BILL BAILEY is based on the last four measures of the song.

BILL BAILEY, WON'T YOU PLEASE COME HOME

Medium Fast
Key of F

Introduction

REPEAT SIGNS

Quite often, a song has more than one set of lyrics, or a part of a song has to be played a second time. Instead of printing that section again, "repeat signs" are used.

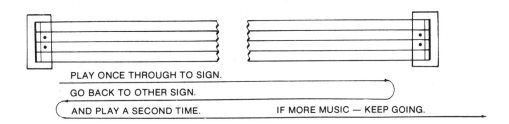

PLAY ONCE THROUGH TO SIGN.
GO BACK TO OTHER SIGN.
AND PLAY A SECOND TIME.   IF MORE MUSIC — KEEP GOING.

DOUBLE ENDINGS

Some songs have more than one ending. In these cases, a "double ending" is used.

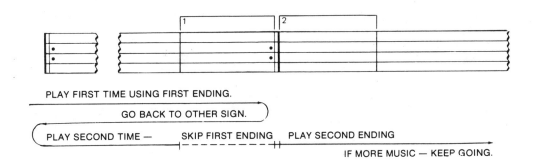

PLAY FIRST TIME USING FIRST ENDING.
GO BACK TO OTHER SIGN.
PLAY SECOND TIME —   SKIP FIRST ENDING   PLAY SECOND ENDING
                                              IF MORE MUSIC — KEEP GOING.

Other things to notice about the arrangement:

1. DANUBE WAVES is written in the key of A minor (CLUE — the last chord symbol in the song usually indicates the key). A minor has the same key signature as C major — no sharps or flats. This makes them "relative keys."

2. The left hand part consists of "pyramid chords" — chords whose notes are played one at a time and held. Practice the accompaniment alone before you play the arrangement.

3. The end of DANUBE WAVES features a type of arpeggio that you've played before. Practice this part separately, using the sustain pedal as indicated.

DANUBE WAVES
(Popular version known as "The Anniversary Song")

Medium Slow
Key of Am

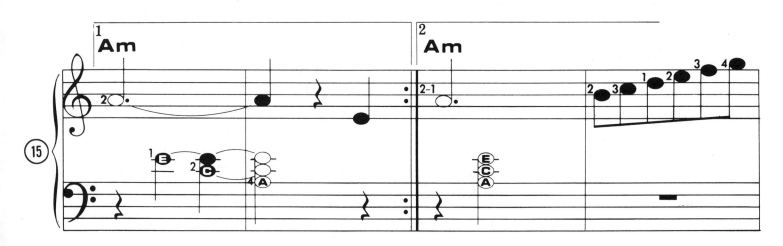

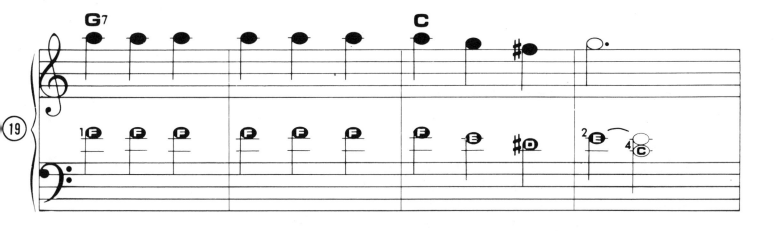

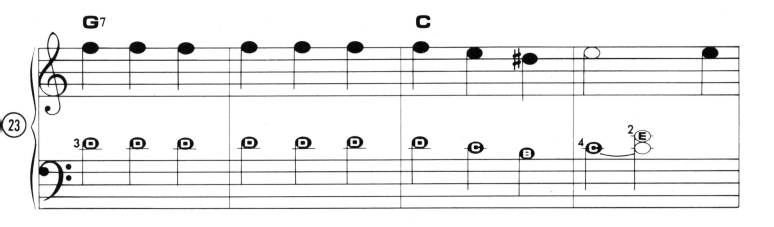

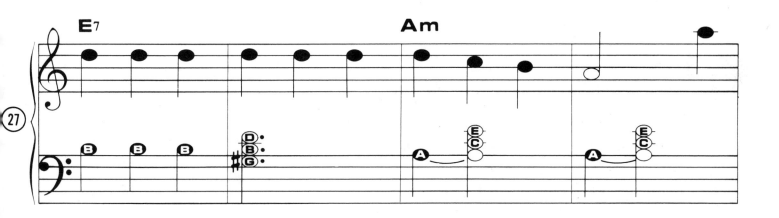

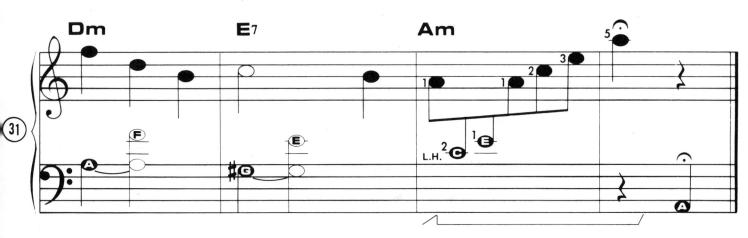

KUMBAYA

DOTTED QUARTER NOTES

RULE: A DOT PLACED AFTER A NOTE INCREASES THE TIME VALUE OF THE NOTE BY ONE-HALF. You saw this applied to the dotted half note (2 beats + 1 beat) back in Part 1; here's how it applies in the case of dotted quarter notes:

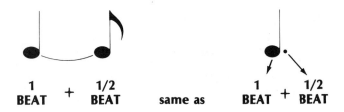

Most often, a dotted quarter note is followed by an eighth note for a total time value of two beats (1-1/2 + 1/2 = 2). This is the way the dotted quarter notes appear in KUMBAYA; the next example shows how counting and foot-taps apply. Play it a few times.

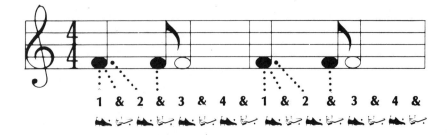

Musicians often refer to this as the "soft rock pattern" when it is repeatedly played by an instrument such as the bass guitar.

Try this excerpt from a well-known song.

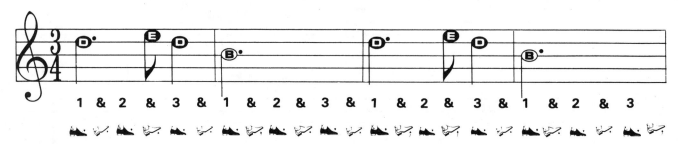

58

KUMBAYA

Medium

Key of C

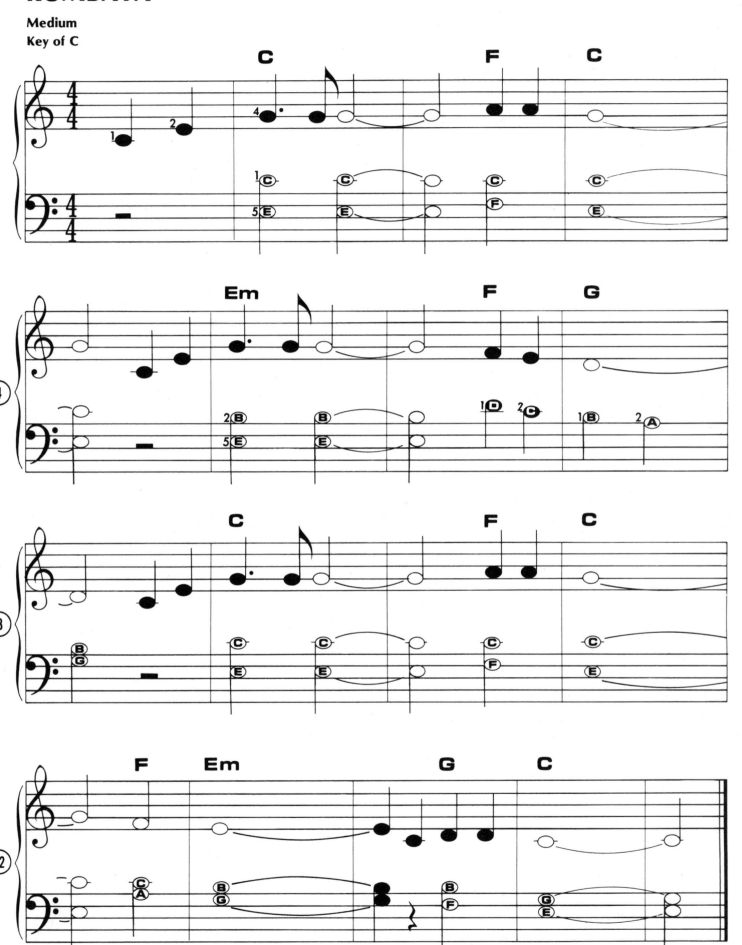

REVIEW

A. NAME THE NOTES

By naming the notes below, you can decode
the message.

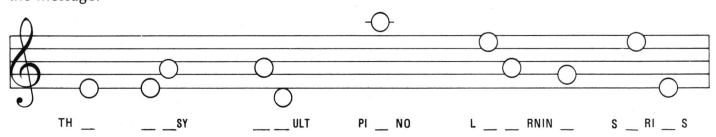

TH __ __ __SY __ __ULT PI __ NO L __ __ RNIN __ S __ RI __ S

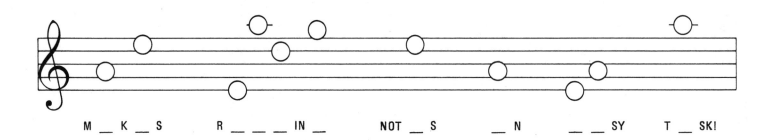

M __ K __ S R __ __ __ IN __ NOT __ S __ N __ __ SY T __ SK!

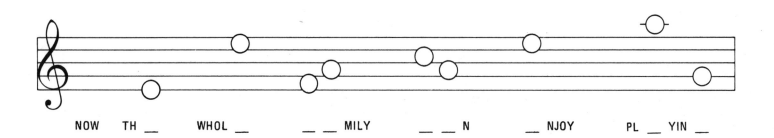

NOW TH __ WHOL __ __ __ MILY __ __ N __ NJOY PL __ YIN __

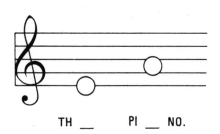

TH __ PI __ NO.

60

B. MATCHING

Match the numbers in the left hand column to the correct answers at the right.

1. Pick-up notes

2. ⌢

3. Octave

4. ♩.

5. Measure

6. ‖: :‖

7. Key signature

8. No sharps or flats

9. ⊕ CODA

10. F major

11. Introduction

12. Relative

13. ♩. ♪♩

14. Scale

15. G major

(　　) Major and minor keys having the same key signature.

(　　) Eight notes apart.

(　　) Notes played before the first chord is played.

(　　) Pause or hold

(　　) Sometimes called the "soft rock" rhythm.

(　　) Space between two bar lines.

(　　) Establishes the mood of a song.

(　　) One sharp in key signature.

(　　) Key of C major.

(　　) Orderly series of notes based on a whole-step/half-step pattern.

(　　) Worth 1-1/2 beats.

(　　) Indicates the scale on which the song is based.

(　　) One flat in key signature.

(　　) Repeat signs.

(　　) Part of a song used as the ending.

ANSWERS:

B. Matching: (12) (3) (1) (2) (13) (5) (11) (8) (15) (14) (4) (7) (10) (6) (9)

A. The Easy Adult Piano Learning Series makes reading notes an easy task! Now the whole family can enjoy playing the piano.

NATURAL ACCENTS

Although the beats occurring in any measure are equal in time value, some of them are played with an accent that makes them stronger than the others; this helps add variety and a rhythmic feel to music. Consider the "OOM-pah-pah" of the waltz rhythm — the first beat is always played with more emphasis than the other two. This makes the first beat in each measure of $\frac{3}{4}$ time a "primary beat"; the other two beats are called "secondary beats." In $\frac{4}{4}$ time, the first and third beats in each measure are considered primary; the second and fourth beats, then, are secondary.

Accent marks (>) help indicate primary beats in the example.

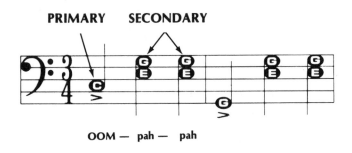

It is the placement of accents that helps music flow rhythmically. It is the placement of accents that also introduces the next subject.

SYNCOPATION

"Syncopation" occurs when accents are placed anywhere but on primary beats.

The examples below show how accented secondary beats helped give a "ragtime" feeling to songs from the turn of the century. Play each melody and strike a bit harder the keys represented by notes marked with accents.

HELLO! MY BABY

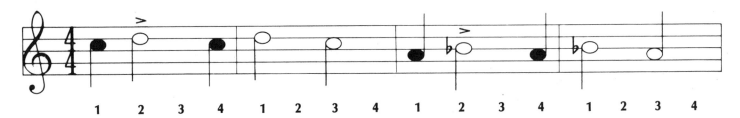

GIVE MY REGARDS TO BROADWAY

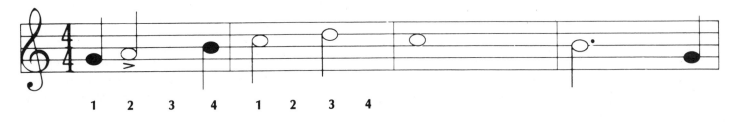

Syncopation also occurs when accents fall BETWEEN the beats in a measure; this is what gives jazz tunes and Latin-American rhythms their distinctive flavors. The first part shows the accents on the primary first and third beats; the second part shows the accents on the first beat and the upbeat ("and") between the second and third beats. The two E notes being tied emphasizes the syncopated feeling when you play. Try it.

UNSYNCOPATED

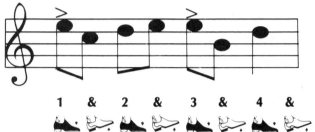

SYNCOPATED

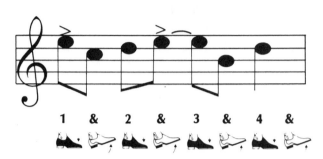

What you're doing in the second part of the example is anticipating the third beat by playing its accent before you actually get to it. You can explore this further by playing the next two examples — the first two measures of THE ENTERTAINER, shown without syncopation, and with.

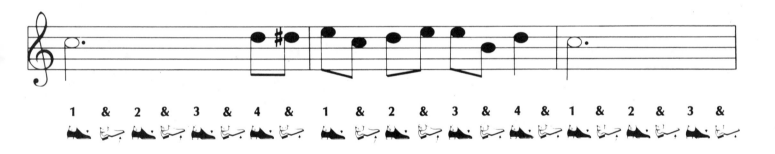

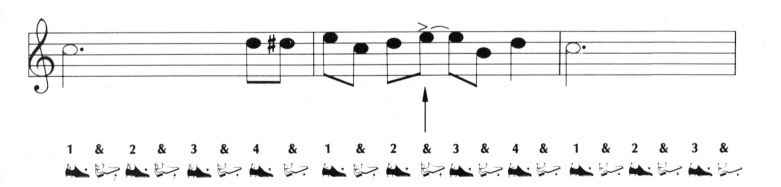

The arrow appearing in the second example is used throughout the arrangement of THE ENTERTAINER to guide you through the places where syncopation occurs. Take your time and play the melody of the song alone at first — then add the left hand part.

THE ENTERTAINER

Medium Fast

Key of C

FRANKIE AND JOHNNY

Medium
Key of C

This song gives you additional practice at playing syncopation. As in the last song, arrows are used throughout to guide you. You may want to write in the counting as shown in the first two measures of the song.

The left hand part of this song is more rhythmic than most of the songs you've played up to now; it will be helpful if you practice it separately at first. Measures 9 through 15 feature an accompaniment style known as "walking bass" — these notes must be played on the beat, especially considering the syncopation that occurs in the melody of the same measures.

HE'S GOT THE WHOLE WORLD IN HIS HANDS

Medium
Key of C

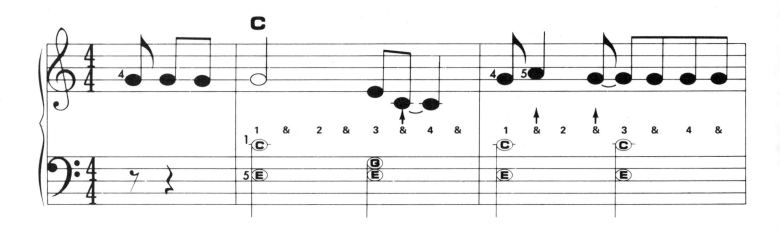

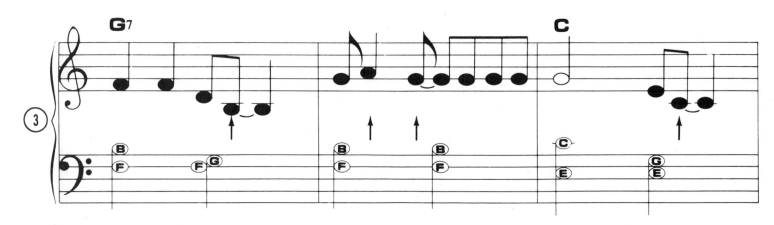

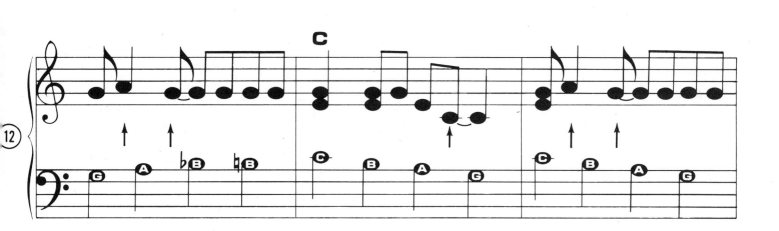

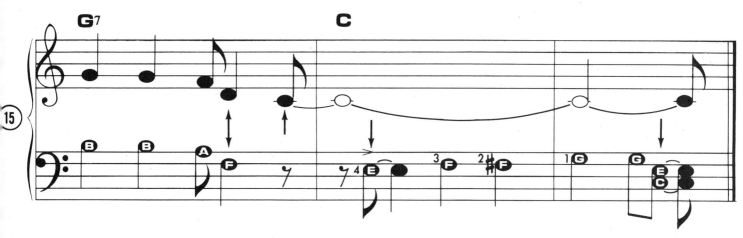

MICHAEL, ROW THE BOAT ASHORE

NEW ACCOMPANIMENT STYLE

In the last few years, the piano has been enjoying renewed interest from musicians and listeners alike. In the popular music field especially, the piano, whether electronic or acoustic, is making its presence known on an ever-increasing number of recordings.

The arrangement of MICHAEL, ROW THE BOAT ASHORE features an accompaniment style that can frequently be heard in current "pop/rock" music. Since this style involves playing left hand notes as far apart as an octave,

you'll find it helpful to play the examples shown here. They're based on the first line of the arrangement. The first example is in half notes, played at the same time, to help you get used to the wider hand positions. After you've played it a few times, try to do it without looking at your keyboard.

The second example is written in quarter notes, played as they are in the song itself; these should be played in a smooth, legato style.

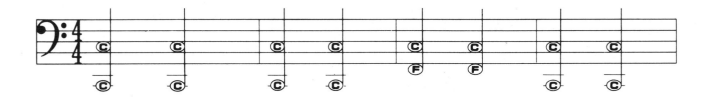

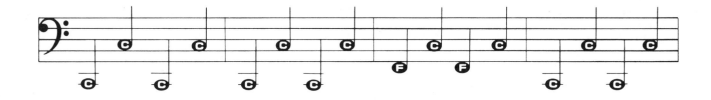

The left hand style is also used in a rather unusual arrangement of WHEN THE SAINTS GO MARCHING OUT (IN), which appears in the "Easy Favorites" section.

MICHAEL, ROW THE BOAT ASHORE

Medium
Key of C

MORE ON INTRODUCTIONS

As you learned in BILL BAILEY, an INTRO-DUCTION prepares the listener for the song itself by establishing the tempo and general mood. Most introductions of today's pop or standard songs, are generally four to eight measures long and are usually taken from the song itself.

Many classical composers, on the other hand, created introductions that were, in themselves, mini-compositions of various lengths — some had moods and themes totally different from any part of the main body of the composition.

Johann Strauss, a famous composer of Viennese waltzes, wrote "Tales from the Vienna Woods." The introduction of this song is fourteen measures long and does establish the tempo and general mood of the song. It's melodic content, however, is not repeated anywhere within the composition.

MODULATION

Modulation is the process of changing from one key (signature) to another in a smooth, logical manner. Generally, it is done to give new life to a song — or a fresh sound — thereby making the arrangement more interesting. This is especially true if the same segment (or entire song) is to be repeated.

A modulation is also used frequently when playing a medley — it offers a smooth transition, or segue, from one song to another.

Many classical compositions contain different melodic themes located in different segments, or movements. "Tales from the Vienna Woods" contains four distinct sections (excluding the "intro"). The first, in the key of D major, starts at measure 15, the second (also in D major) at measure 43, which acts as a "bridge" into the last two segments starting at measures 58 and 75.

The song sounds as though it could actually end in measure 54. However, the composer may have had a fresh idea for a new melody that would better conclude the song. Measures 55, 56 and 57 contain a "chord prograssion" (a sequence of chords) that segues into the last segment in the key of G major.

TALES FROM THE VIENNA WOODS

Medium
Key of D

72

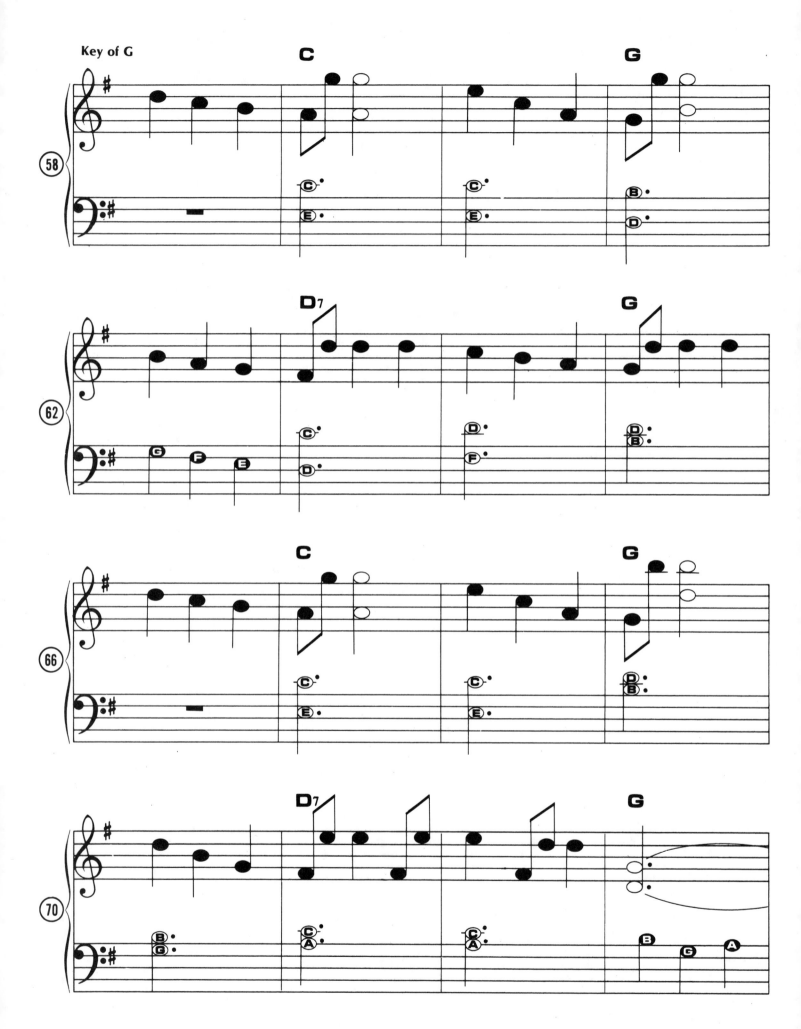

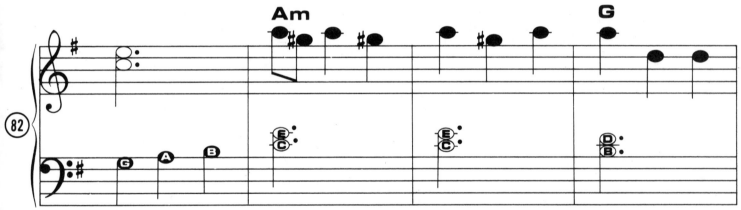

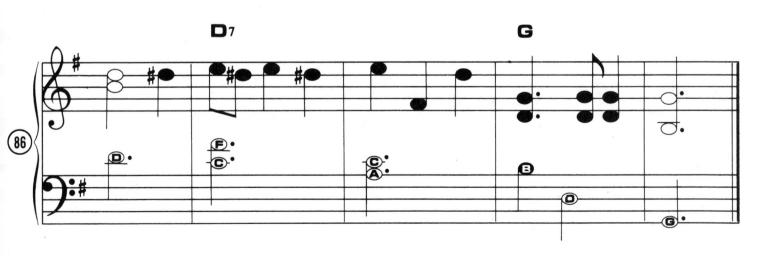

TOYLAND

This arrangement helps you create a charming music box effect. Before you play, however, there are several things you should take note of in your music:

1. The melody is played an octave higher than written throughout the arrangement.

2. The entire left hand part appears on a treble staff — this allows you to more easily play the accompaniment on a higher-sounding part of the keyboard. Letter-names are included to guide you.

3. The accompaniment includes several different playing styles — broken chords, pyramid chords, single notes — be sure to

practice this part alone before you play the entire song.

4. You might also want to practice separately measures 13 and 14 of the melody.

5. At the end of the arrangement, below the bass staff, you'll see the marking "rit." — this is an abbreviation for "ritardando," an Italian word meaning to "gradually slow down." As you play the notes in the arpeggio, you can create the effect of a music box running down.

6. Fermatas appear in measures 28 and 32.

7. Be sure to observe suggested fingering.

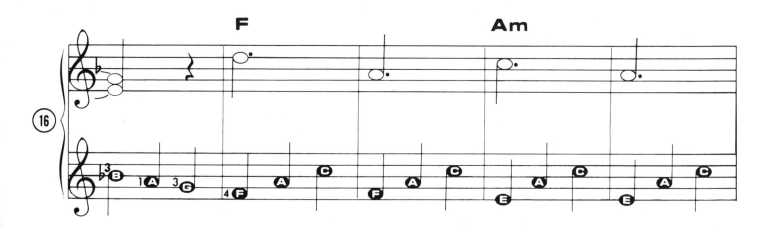

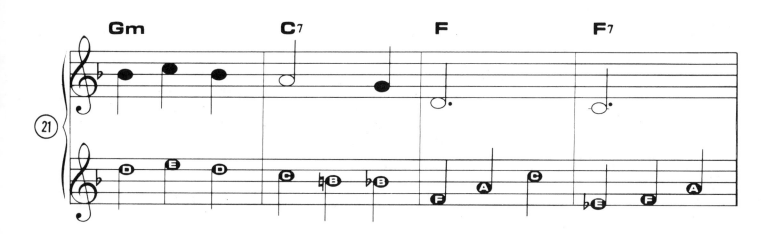

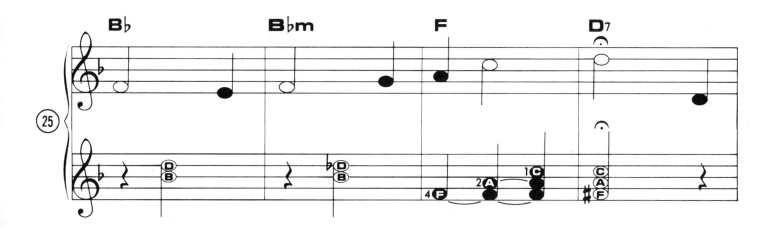

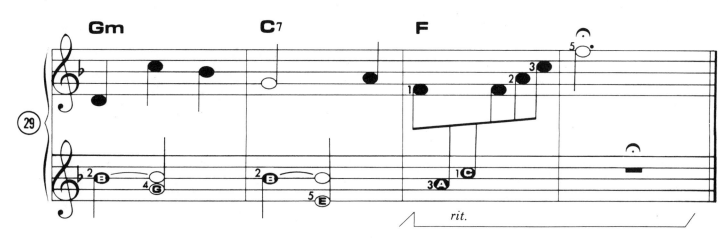

rit.

EIGHTH NOTE TRIPLETS

A triplet is a group of three notes played in the same amount of time it would take to play two notes of the same type. It's easy to recognize the triplet because the three notes usually have a number 3 over the middle note.

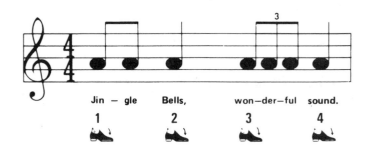

The illustration shows how all eighth note triplets should be counted in relation to other types of notes. Start by tapping your foot slowly and saying the words — then tap your foot and play in the same rhythm as the lyric.

Practice the exercise shown below.

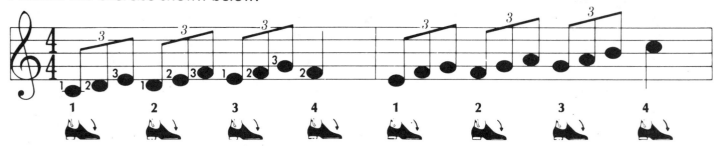

MOZART'S THEME
(Popular version known as "In An Eighteenth Century Drawing Room")

Medium Fast
Key of C

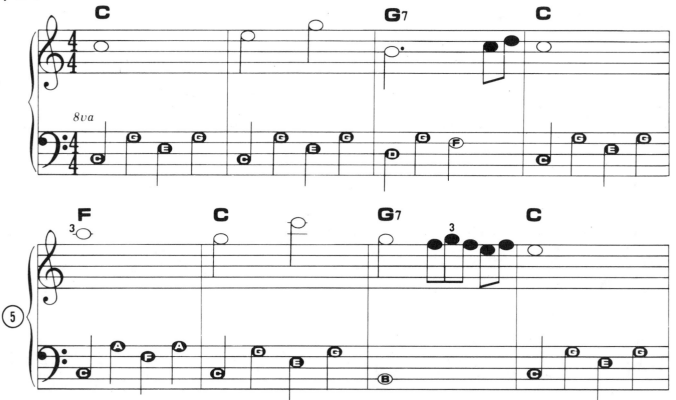

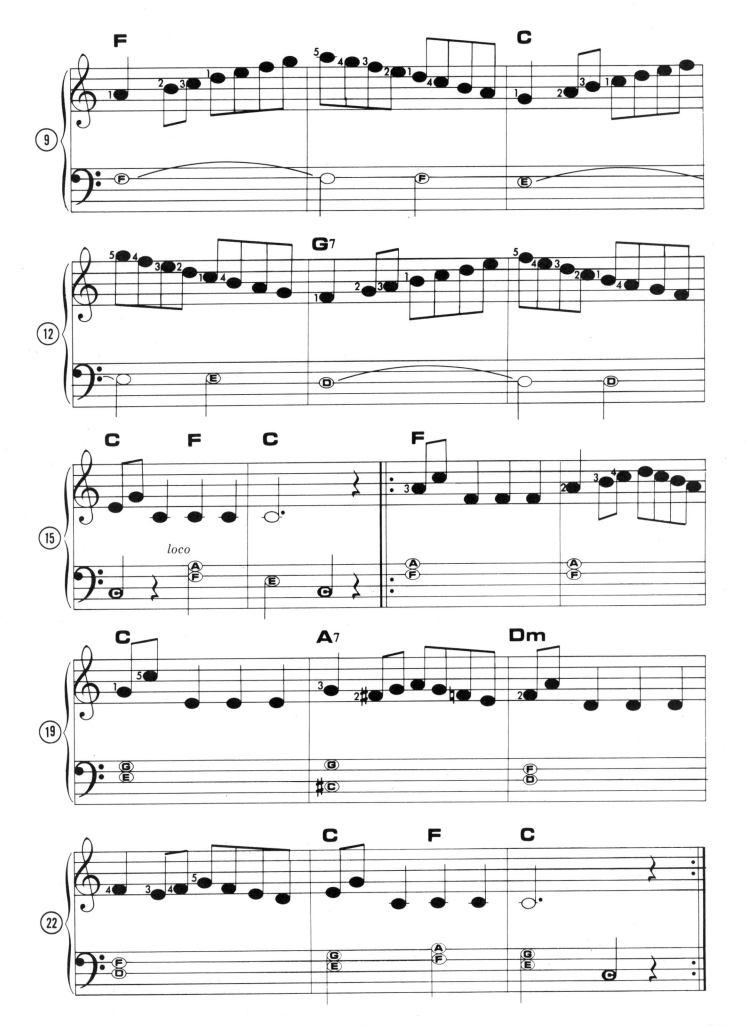

SIXTEENTH NOTES

The time value of a sixteenth note is one-half that of an eighth note and one-fourth that of a quarter note. You already know each beat can be divided into two equal parts — a number and the word "and."

When you count sixteenth notes, each beat may be divided into four equal parts. Each part is indicated by a separate syllable.

Play the example slowly while counting aloud and tapping your foot. Play four sixteenth notes to each foot tap. Make sure you can play them evenly and without hesitation.

INDIVIDUAL SIXTEENTH NOTES (TWO FLAGS)

1 - ah - & - ah - 2 - ah - & - ah - 3 - ah - & - ah - 4 - ah - & - ah -

DOTTED EIGHTH AND SIXTEENTH NOTES

Since an eighth note has a time value of one half-beat, a dot after an eighth note adds one half of that time value (one fourth-beat) to it. Therefore, the total time value of a dotted eighth note equals three-fourths of one beat.

When a dotted eighth note occurs in music, it is usually followed by a sixteenth note. The combined value of these two notes is equivalent to one beat. When this combination of notes appears on a song sheet, the stems are connected by a bar, and the sixteenth note has a small bar attached to its tem, representing the second flag.

A complete measure in 4/4 time, containing the dotted eighth note — sixteenth note pattern, would be counted as shown. The effect is similar to a gallop.

1 ah & ah   2 ah & ah   3 ah & ah   4 ah & ah
ONE BEAT   ONE BEAT   ONE BEAT   ONE BEAT

QUARTER NOTE TRIPLETS

Earlier, you learned that eighth note triplets are played in the same time it takes to play two notes of the same type. This same principle applies to quarter note triplets, which have the same time value as two quarter notes, that is, two beats.

The figure shows how to count quarter note triplets. While tapping your foot in a slow, even tempo, and counting aloud, play the first measure. When you reach the second measure, play the first note on the first downbeat (foot tap). Here's a rule to remember: The first note of a quarter note triplet is ALWAYS played on a beat. The second note is played just before, and the third note is played just after the second beat.

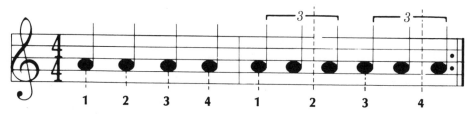

1   2   3   4   1   2   3   4

OTHER TIME SIGNATURES

All the music you've played up to now has had a time signature of either $\frac{3}{4}$ or $\frac{4}{4}$. There are many other time signatures used in music, however. $\frac{6}{8}$ means there are six beats in each measure and every **eighth note** gets **one beat**. The natural accents are on beats 1 and 4. $\frac{3}{8}$ means, three beats in every measure and an eight note gets one beat. This is counted the same as $\frac{3}{4}$ time with the natural accent on beat 1.

With an 8 on the bottom of a time signature, all note values are doubled (as opposed to a 4) i.e., an eighth note gets one beat; quarter note two; half note four; dotted half 6, etc.

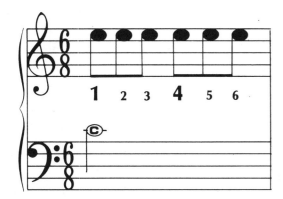

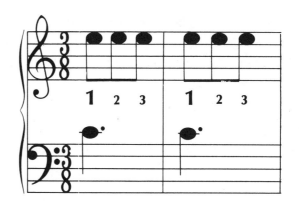

MUSIC GLOSSARY

Most of the following are either traditional markings to help add expression to your playing, or standard musical definitions.

A Tempo — Return to original tempo.

Accelerando (*accel.*) — Increase tempo.

Arpeggio ({) — Symbol appearing before a chord tells you to play one note at a time from lowest to highest.

Crescendo (*cresc.* or ⊂) — Gradually louder.

Da Capo (*D.C.*) — "From the beginning." A type of repeat.

Da Capo al Fine (*D.C. al fine*) — Repeat from beginning to the end (*Fine*).

Dal Segno (*D.S.*) — "From the sign." (𝄋). A type of repeat.

Dal Segno al Fine (*D.S. al fine*) — Repeat from the sign (𝄋) to the end (*Fine*).

Dal Segno al Coda (*D.S. al ⊕ coda*) — Repeat from the sign (𝄋) to where coda sign (⊕) appears; go right to coda.

Decrescendo (*decresc.* or ⊃) — Gradually soften.

Diminuendo (*dim.*) — Same as *decrescendo*.

Dolce — Play smoothly, sweetly

Double bar — Two vertical lines appearing at the end of a section ▦ or of a song ▦

Double Flat (♭♭) — Lowers a tone two half steps.

Double sharp (𝄪) — Raises a tone two half steps.

Dynamics — Contrasts in volume.

Enharmonic tones — Tones having the same pitch but are notated differently, e.g. F♯ and G♭

Expression — Your own touch added to music by variations in volume, touch and, sometimes, tempo.

Expressivo — "With expression."

Fermata — Hold the note longer than its time value.

Fine — The end.

Forte (_f_) — Loud.

Fortissimo (_ff_) — Very loud.

Glissando (_gliss._) — Sliding rapidly from one key to another, playing all keys between.

Grandioso — Play majestically, grandly.

Interval — The distance between any two notes, measured in steps and half steps.

Legato — Play smoothly, connected notes. Opposite of _staccato_.

Loco — Cancels _8va_ sign. Play music as written.

Maestoso — See Grandioso

Mezzo forte (_mf_) — Moderately loud.

Mezzo piano (_mp_) — Moderately soft.

Modulate — Changing key signatures within a song.

Note — The written symbol of a tone.

Octave — 8 notes

Octave higher (_8va_ or 8······⌐ placed above the music) — Play notes one octave higher than written.

Octave lower (_8va_ or 8········⌐ placed below the music) — Play notes one octave lower than written.

Pause (//) — A brief break in the music.

Piano (_p_) — Soft.

Pianissimo (_pp_) — Very Soft.

Pitch — The highness or lowness of a tone.

Poco a poco — "Little by little," or very gradually.

Portamento (● ●) — Slightly disconnected notes.

Rallentando (_rall._) — Gradually slow the tempo.

Ritardando (_rit._) — Same as Rallentando.

Rubato — Variations in tempo allowed. Played freely.

Sempre — Always

Sforzando (_sfz_) — Heavy accent, stronger than (>). Attack loudly and diminish quickly.

Simile — Play in a similar manner.

Slur (● ⌒ ●) — Curved line tells you to play notes smoothly and in a connected manner.

Staccato (♩ ♩ ♩) — "Separate." Play in a detached, light manner.

Tempo — "Time." The speed at which a song is played.

COMMON TEMPO MARKS:
largo — Very slow and broad.
lento — Slow
adagio — Slow, but not as slow as _lento_.
andante — Medium slow.
moderato — Medium speed.

allegretto — Medium fast.
allegro — Quite fast.
presto — Very fast.
vivace — Lively.

Tone — A sound with a definite pitch.

CHORD CHART
CHORDS USED IN PART 2

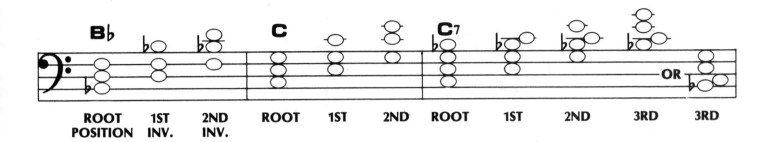

Bb — ROOT POSITION · 1ST INV. · 2ND INV.
C — ROOT · 1ST · 2ND
C7 — ROOT · 1ST · 2ND · 3RD · 3RD

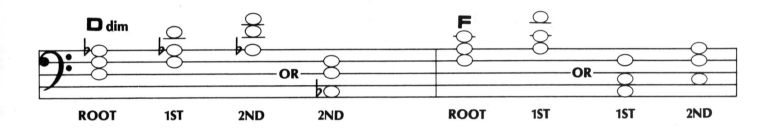

Ddim — ROOT · 1ST · 2ND · 2ND
F — ROOT · 1ST · 1ST · 2ND

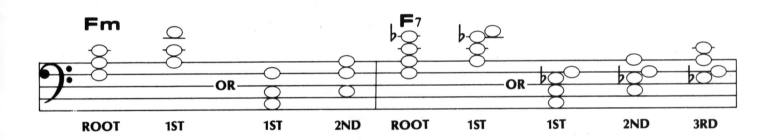

Fm — ROOT · 1ST · OR · 1ST · 2ND
F7 — ROOT · 1ST · OR · 1ST · 2ND · 3RD

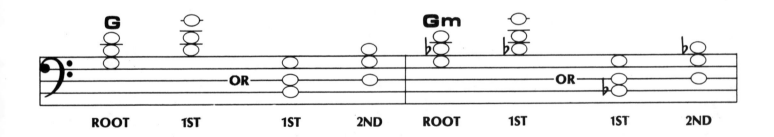

G — ROOT · 1ST · OR · 1ST · 2ND
Gm — ROOT · 1ST · OR · 1ST · 2ND

AULD LANG SYNE

MEDIUM FAST
KEY OF F

AULD LANG SYNE

MEDIUM FAST
KEY OF F

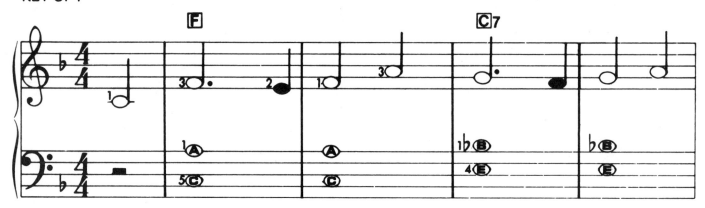

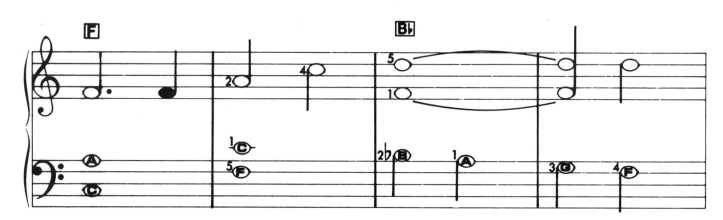

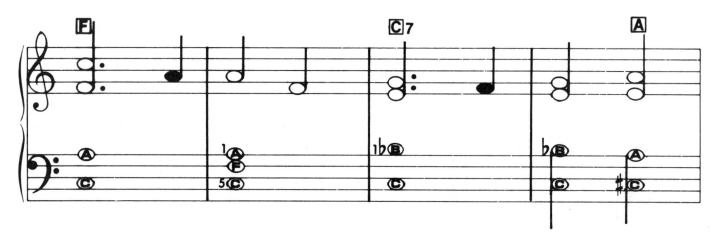

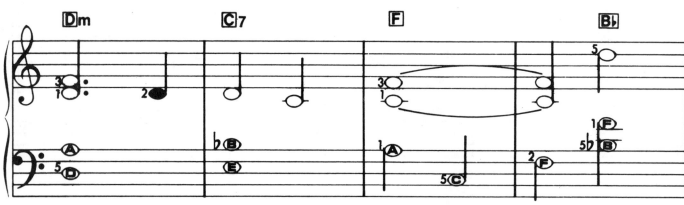

EASY BEGINNER

JINGLE BELLS

MEDIUM FAST
KEY OF F

JINGLE BELLS

MEDIUM FAST
KEY OF F

EASY BEGINNER

HARK!
THE HERALD ANGELS SING

MEDIUM FAST
KEY OF F

HARK!
THE HERALD ANGELS SING

MEDIUM FAST
KEY OF F

EASY BEGINNER

SILENT NIGHT

SLOW
KEY OF C

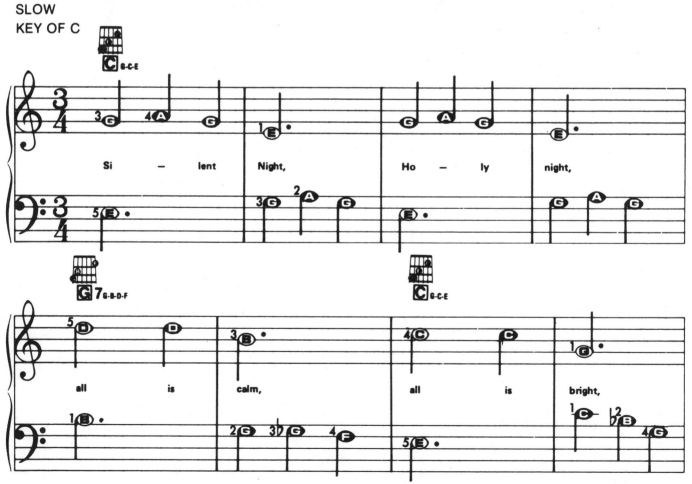

SILENT NIGHT

SLOW
KEY OF C

BEAUTIFUL BROWN EYES

BEAUTIFUL BROWN EYES

THEME
"FROM THE NEW WORLD"
SYMPHONY

SLOW

THEME
"FROM THE NEW WORLD"
SYMPHONY

EASY PRO

SLOW

MARIANNE

MEDIUM

MARIANNE

MEDIUM

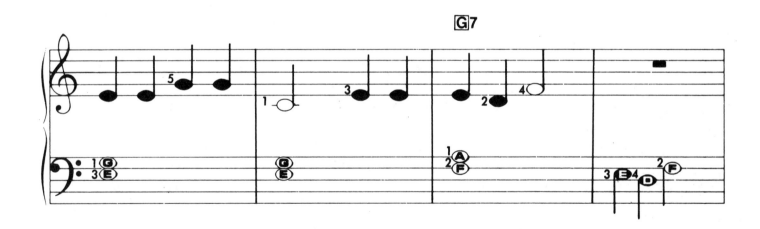

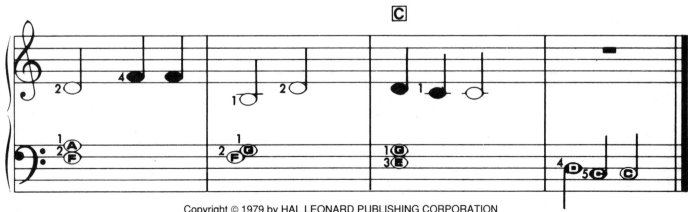

EASY BEGINNER

LONG, LONG AGO

MEDIUM SLOW
KEY OF C

Now you are here all my grief is re — moved.

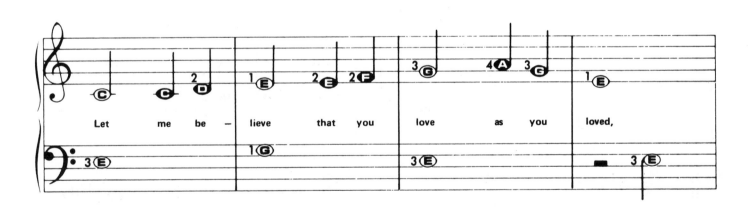

Let me for — get that so long you have roved.

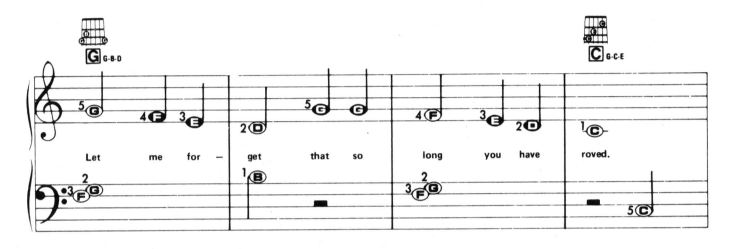

Let me be — lieve that you love as you loved,

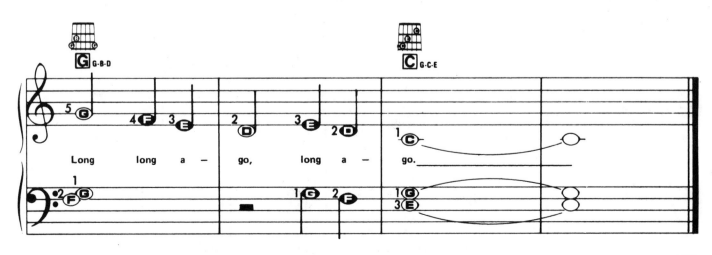

Long long a — go, long a — go.

LONG, LONG AGO

MEDIUM SLOW
KEY OF C

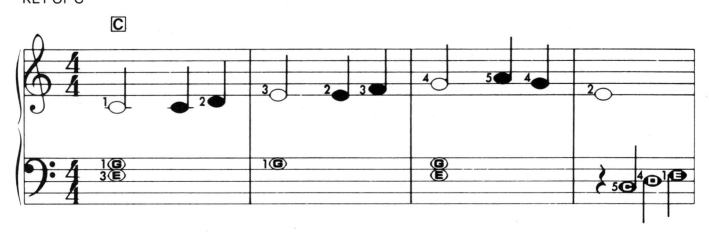

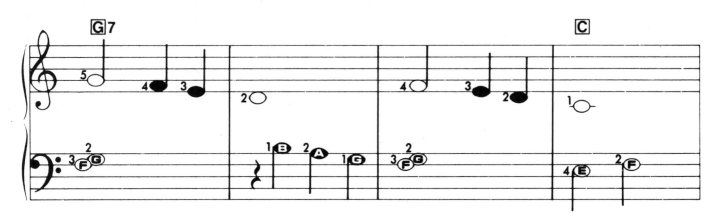

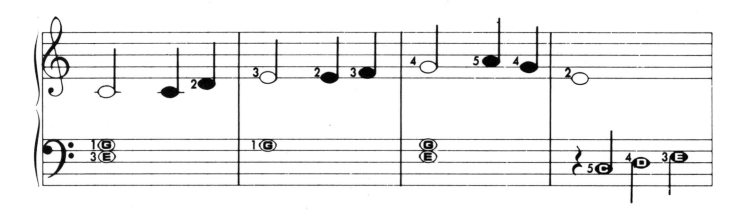

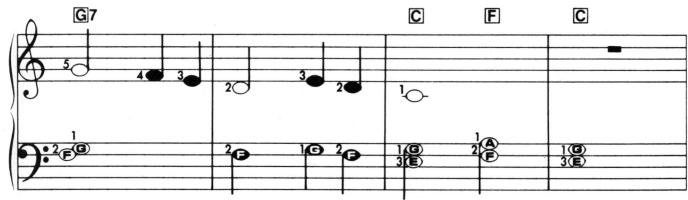

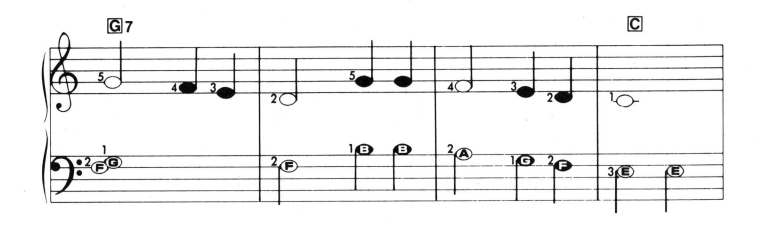

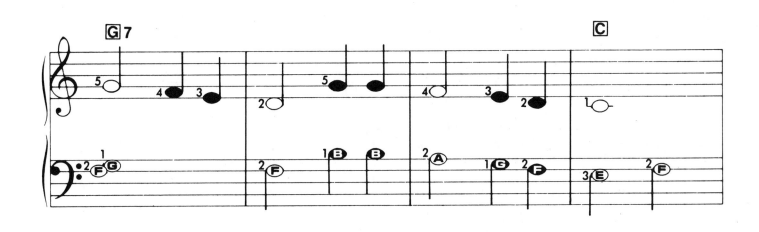

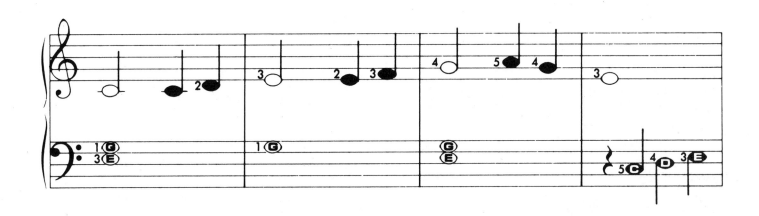

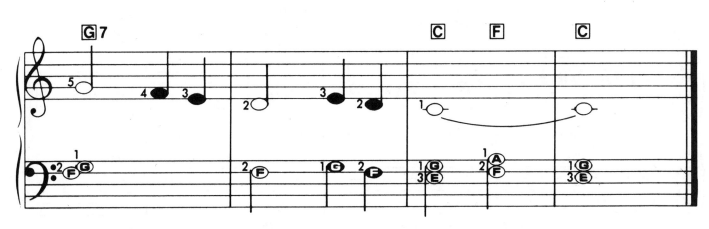

AURA LEE
(Popular version known as "Love Me Tender")

SLOW

KEY OF G

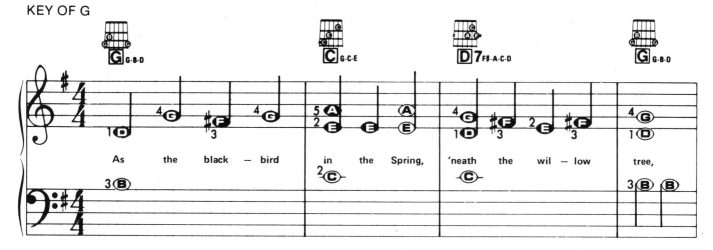

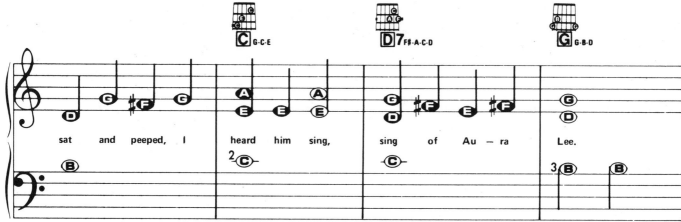

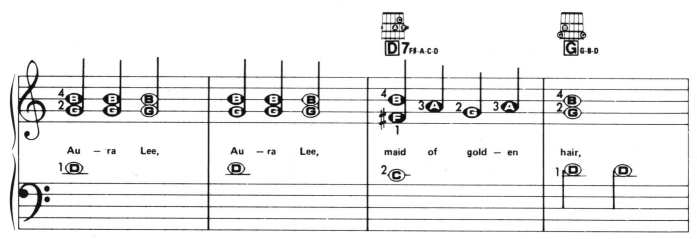

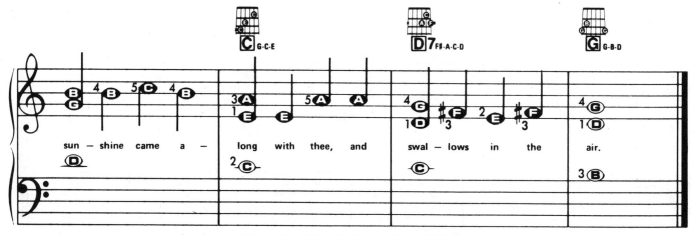

AURA LEE
(Popular version known as "Love Me Tender")

EASY PRO

SLOW

KEY OF G

LAVENDER'S BLUE

EASY BEGINNER

MEDIUM
KEY OF C

LAVENDER'S BLUE

MEDIUM
KEY OF C

I LOVE YOU TRULY

MEDIUM SLOW
KEY OF C

MELODY OF LOVE

SLOW

KEY OF F

MELODY OF LOVE

SLOW

KEY OF F

EASY BEGINNER

SCARBOROUGH FAIR

MEDIUM SLOW
KEY OF Am

SCARBOROUGH FAIR

MEDIUM SLOW
KEY OF Am

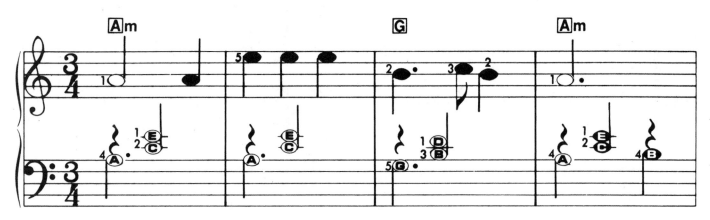

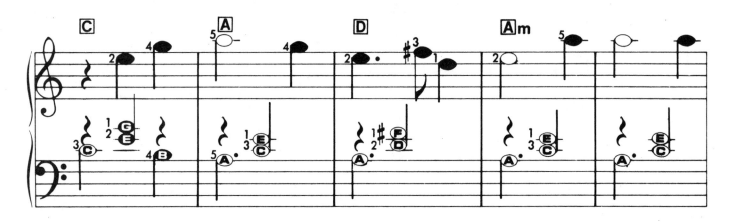

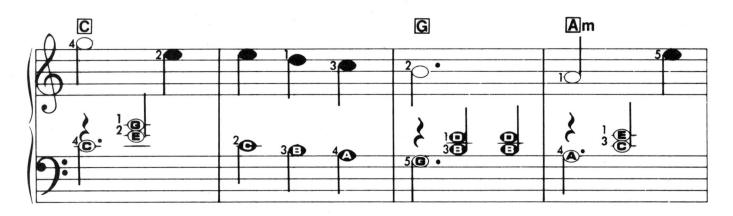

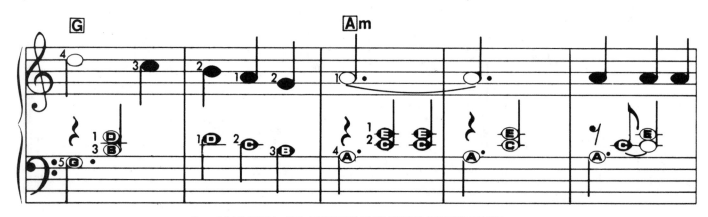

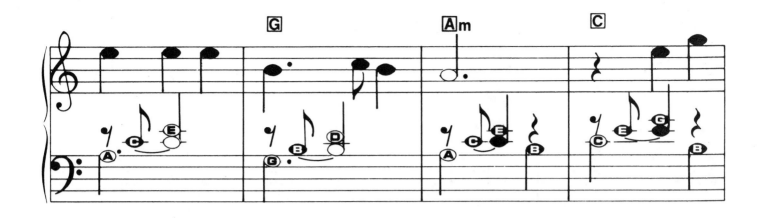

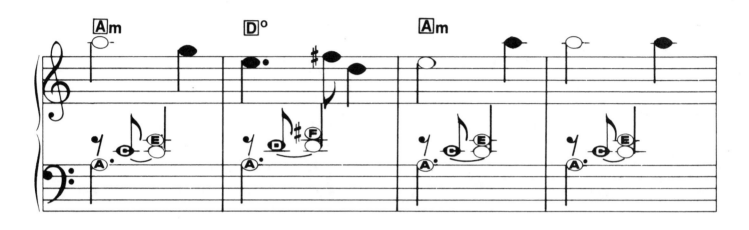

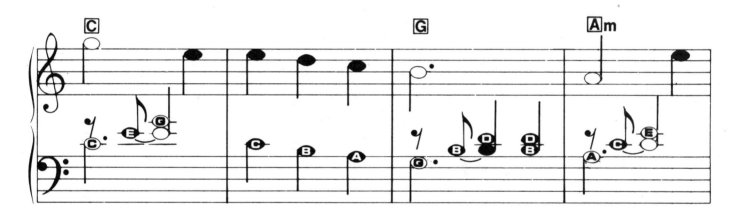

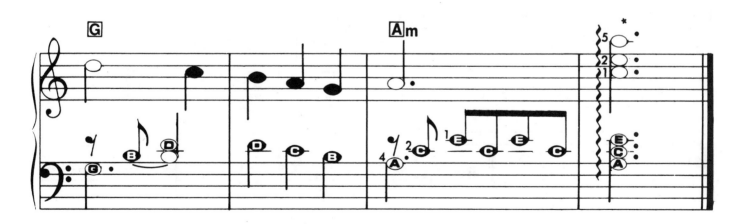

*Arpeggio—Play notes one-at-a-time very quickly from lowest to highest.
The effect is that of strumming a chord on a guitar.

EASY BEGINNER

CAN-CAN

(From "Orpheus in the Underworld")

MEDIUM FAST
KEY OF C

CAN-CAN
(From "Orpheus in the Underworld")

MEDIUM FAST
KEY OF C

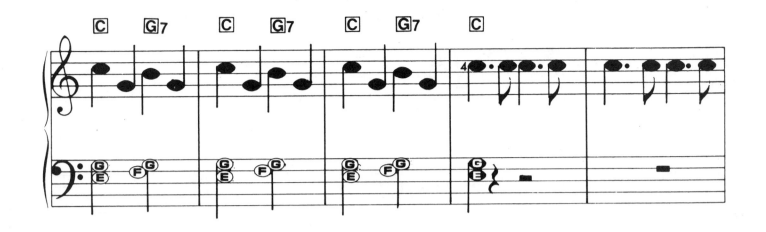

KEY OF F

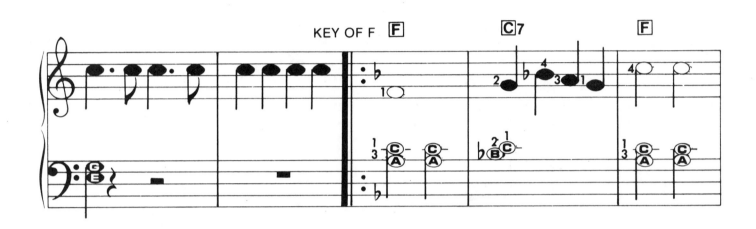

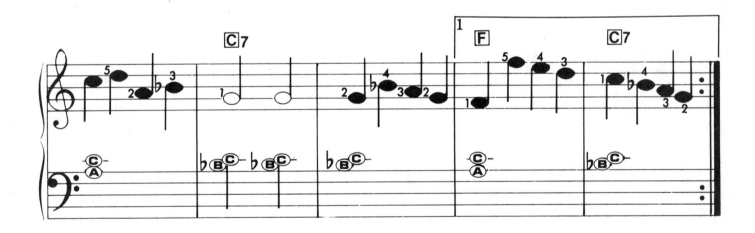

KEY OF C

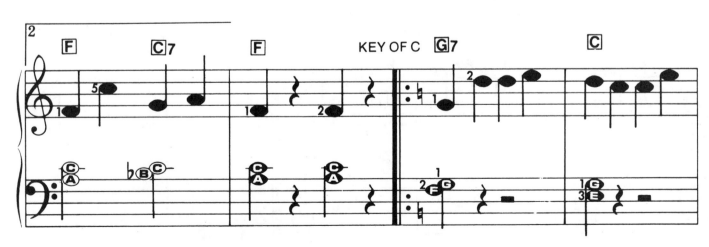

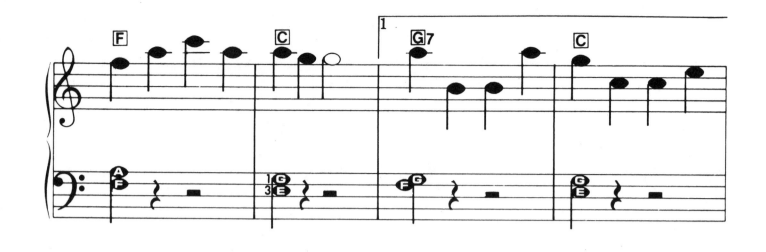

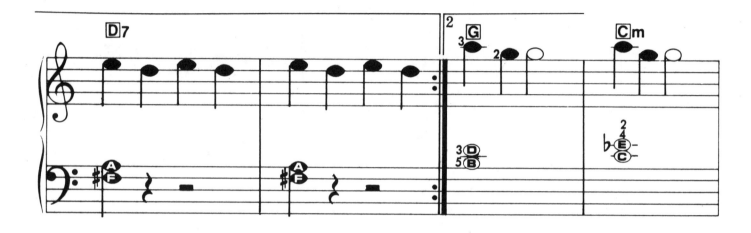

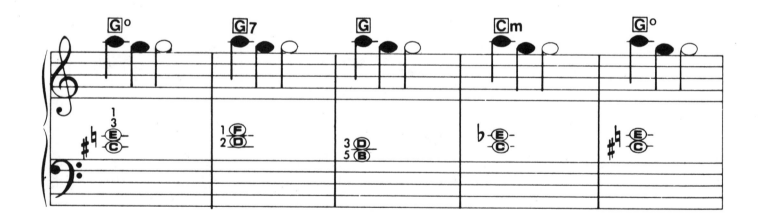

128

TREBLE CLEF

BASS CLEF

WHEN THE SAINTS
GO MARCHING OUT (IN)

MEDIUM FAST
KEY OF C MINOR

*(see footnote)

(Bagpipe effect)

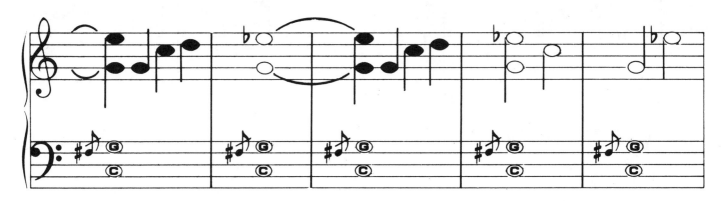

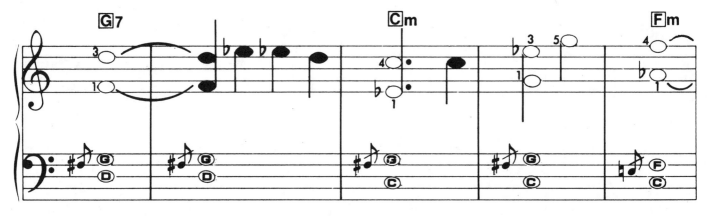

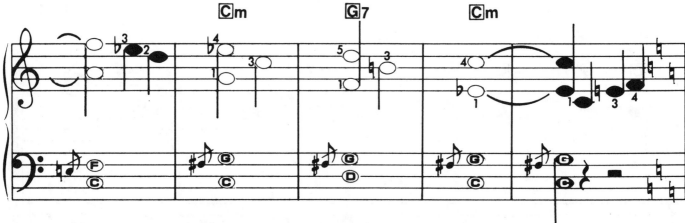

*Grace notes (optional)—Grace notes have no actual time value. They're used to "decorate" or "embellish" the note(s) immediately following. Play them as quickly as possible.

KEY OF C MAJOR

EASY BEGINNER

LONDONDERRY AIR
(Popular version known as "Danny Boy")

SLOW

KEY OF F

LONDONDERRY AIR

(Popular version known as "Danny Boy")

SLOW

KEY OF F

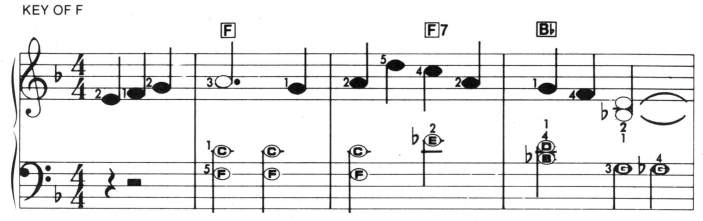

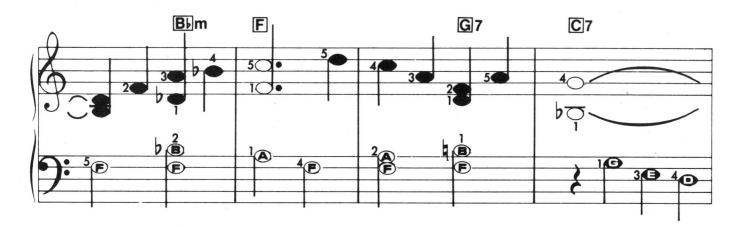

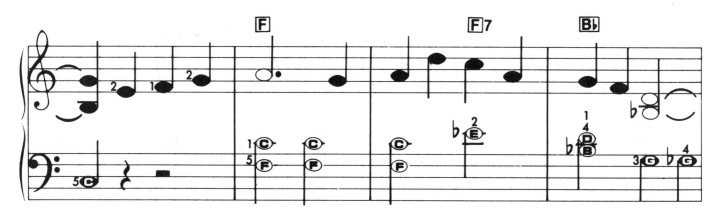

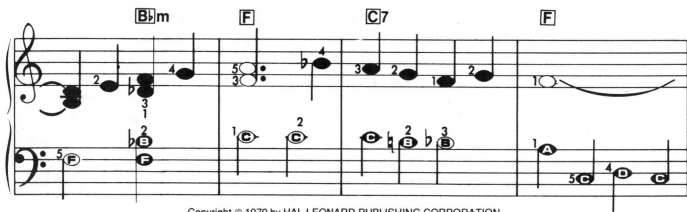

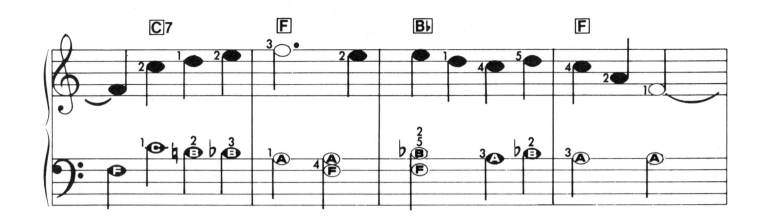

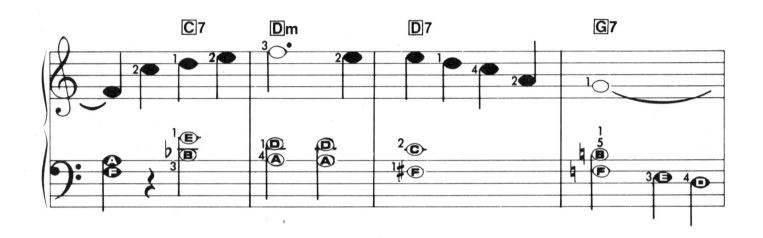

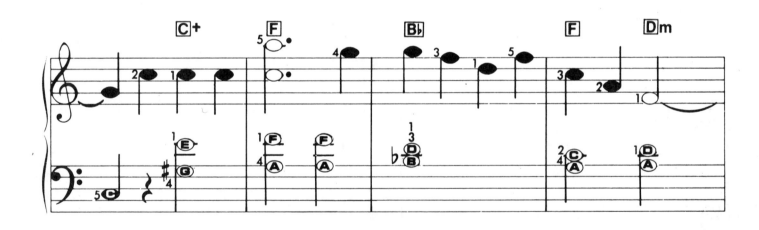

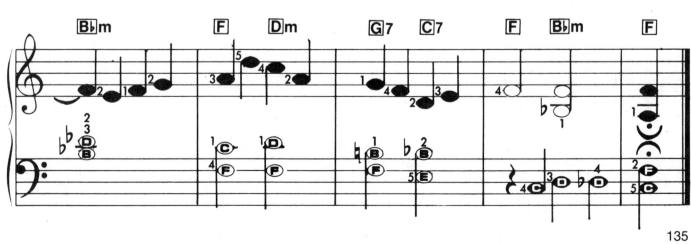

GYPSY LOVE SONG

EASY BEGINNER

MEDIUM

KEY OF C

GYPSY LOVE SONG

MEDIUM
KEY OF C

Notice that the lower staff is written in TREBLE clef. This is to eliminate the three ledger lines that would be needed if written in bass clef. The bottom staff is still played with the left hand.

138

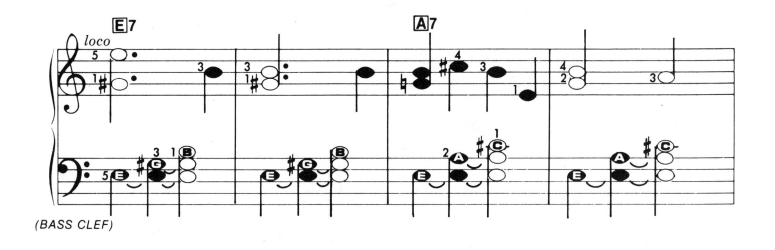

(BASS CLEF)

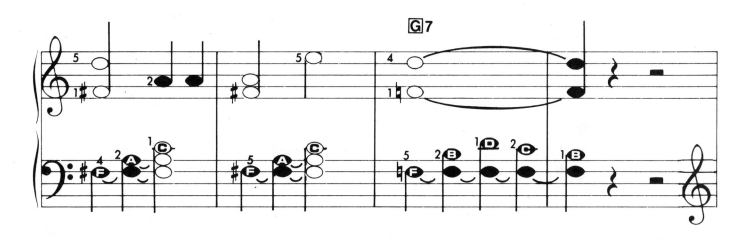

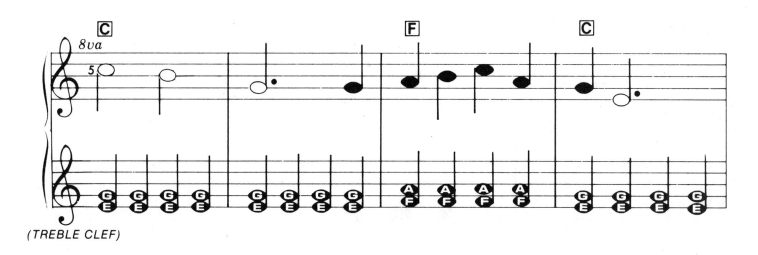

(TREBLE CLEF)

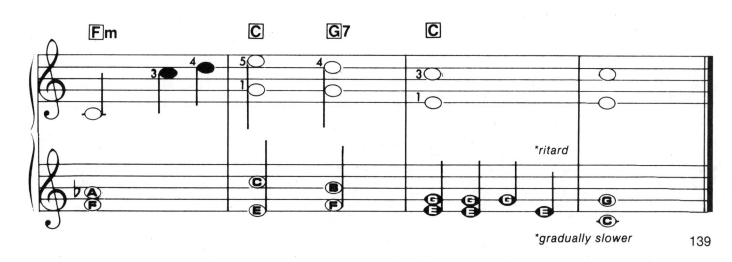

*ritard

*gradually slower

139

EASY BEGINNER

FASCINATION

MEDIUM SLOW

KEY OF C

141

FASCINATION

MEDIUM SLOW

KEY OF C

142

EASY BEGINNER

TO A WILD ROSE

SLOW AND TENDERLY
KEY OF F

(TREBLE CLEF)

(BASS CLEF)

TO A WILD ROSE

SLOW AND TENDERLY
KEY OF F

*The 4 indicates the addition of the 4th note of the C scale; in this case, the F.

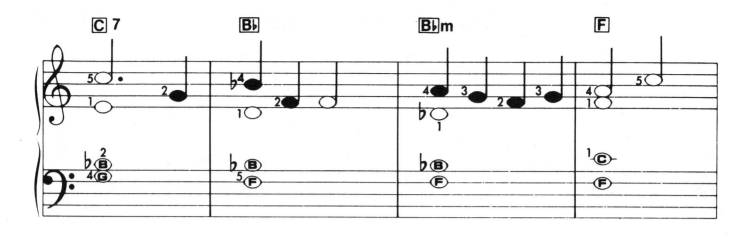

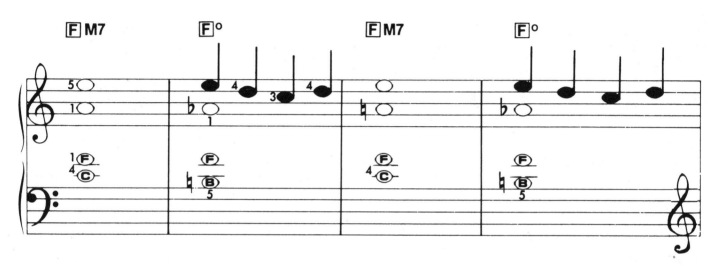

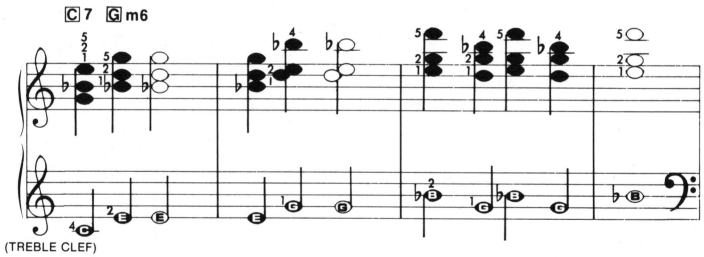

(TREBLE CLEF)

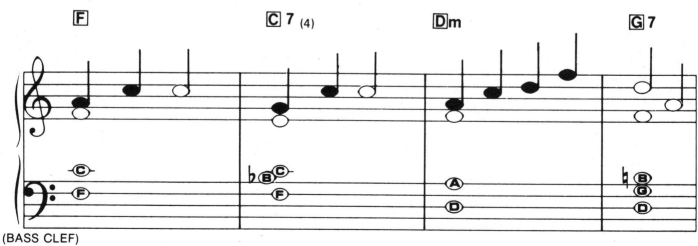

(BASS CLEF)

*Hold pedal until sound completely fades away.

SKATERS WALTZ

MEDIUM FAST
KEY OF C

EASY PRO

SKATERS WALTZ

MEDIUM FAST
KEY OF C

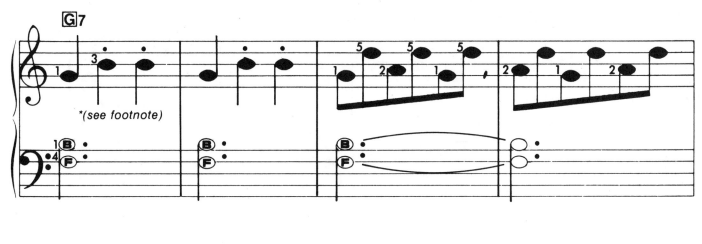

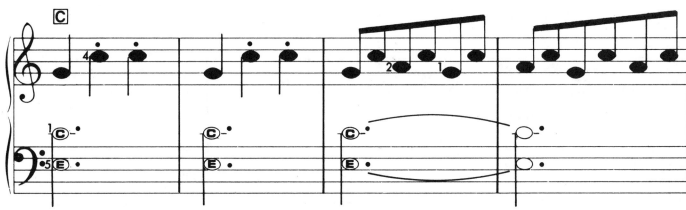

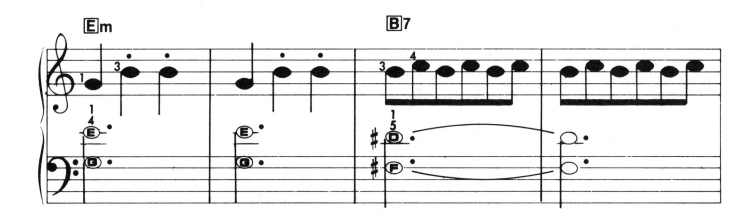

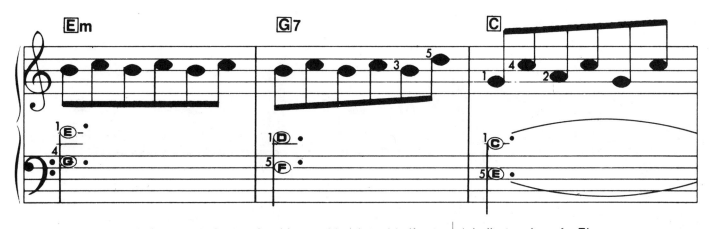

*A dot placed **above** or **below** a note (not to the side, as with a dotted-half note ♩.), indicates **staccato.** The note is played very **short**—strike and release the key **instantly.** The results can be compared to playing eighth notes followed by eighth rests:

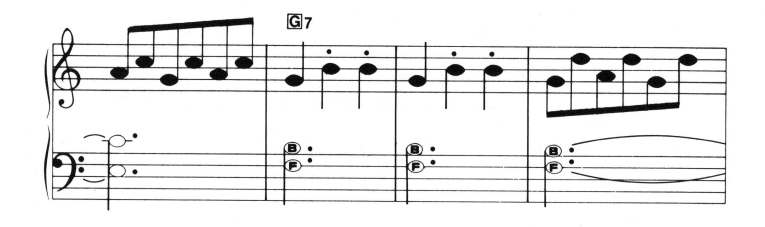

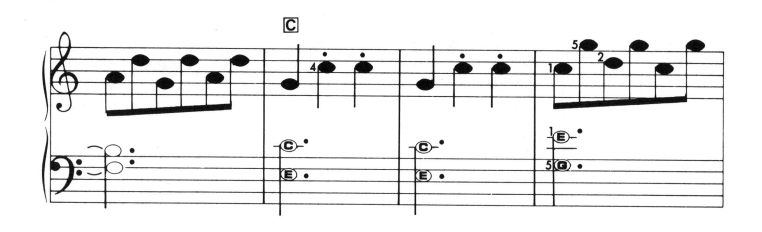

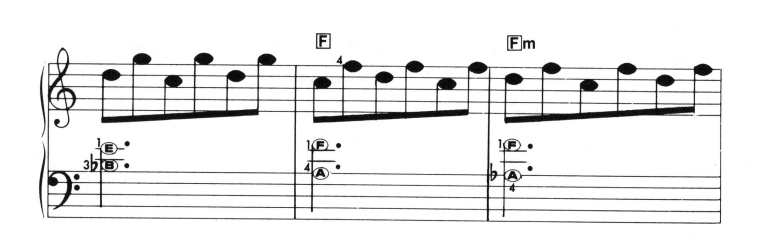

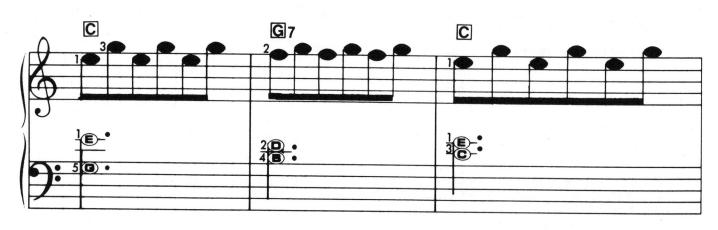

156

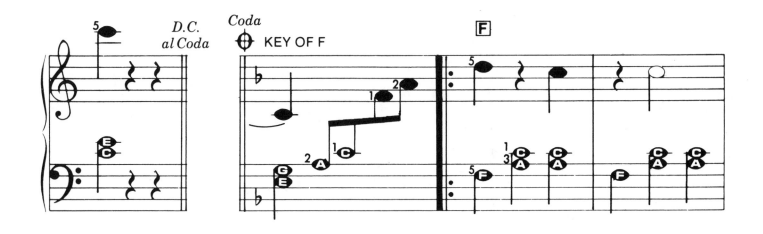

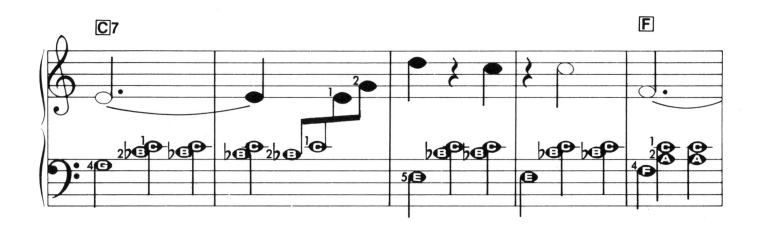

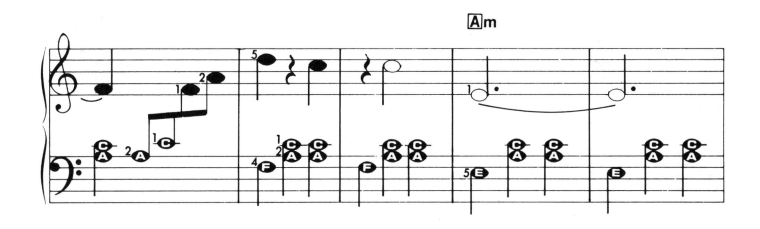

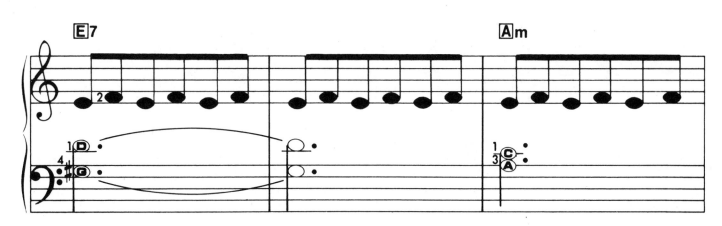

157

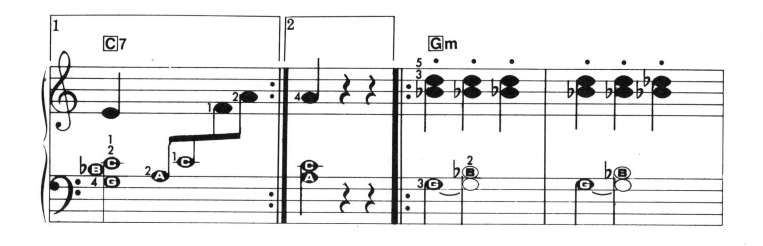

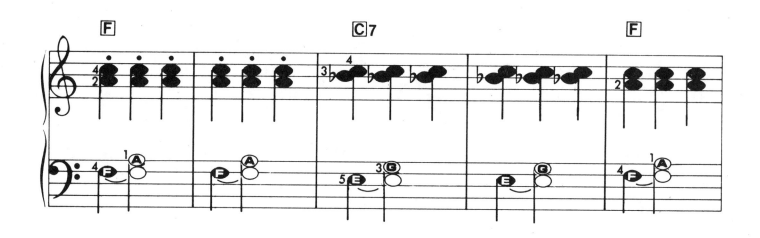

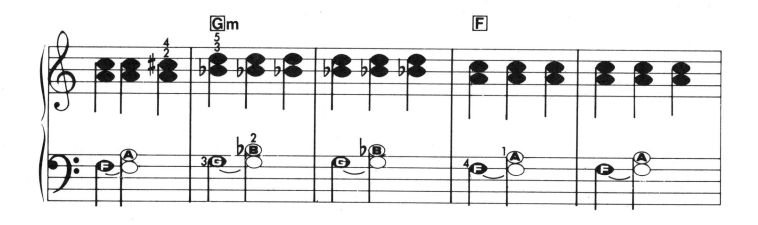

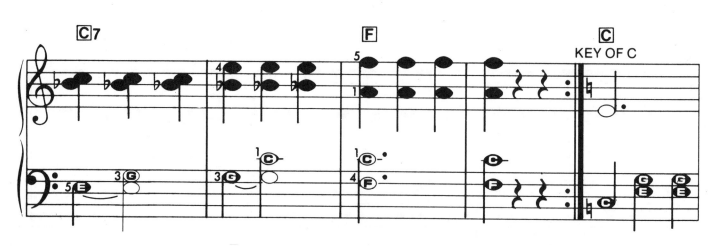

*Octaves are optional—only the top or bottom notes may be played.

159

*Octaves are optional.

160

EASY ADULT Piano

These books, for all acoustic and electronic pianos, feature professional piano arrangements designed for amateur adult pianists. They're easy to read and easy to play so even beginners can play their favorite songs quickly, easily, and well. Chord symbols are included for use with the automatic chord feature found on many portable keyboards and electronic keyboards. Basic directions help the player get started.

EASY ADULT PIANO BEGINNER'S COURSE
160 pages of step-by-step piano instruction that begins in easy A-B-C notation in the treble clef and easy play in the bass clef. Over 40 songs, including: Greensleeves • Scarborough Fair • The Entertainer • Mozart's Theme. Professionally arranged to make adult beginners sound great and inspire them to continue to learn. A-B-C stickers included.
00001101 . . . .$14.95

PIANO IN THE DARK AND OTHER SOFT HITS
Arranged by Joe Raposo
15 songs: Don't You Know What The Night Can Do • Make Me Lose Control • Moonlighting • Piano In The Dark • On My Own and more.
00001490 . . . .$7.95

PIANO CLASSICS
Arranged by Joe Raposo
22 favorites, including Claire de Lune by Debussy • Fleur de Lis by Beethoven • Liebestraum by Liszt • Polonaise by Chopin • Romeo And Juliet by Tchaikovsky • Tales From The Vienna Woods by Strauss and more.
00001022 . . . .$7.95

CLASSIC LOVE SONGS
17 sentimental favorites, including: All The Things You Are • Endless Love • I Will Always Love You • Just The Way You Are • Save The Best For Last • Somewhere Out There • When I Fall In Love • A Whole New World • and more.
00243164 . . . .$7.95

COUNTRY HITS
20 songs, including: Achy Breaky Heart • Boot Scootin' Boogie • Chattahoochee • Forever And Ever, Amen • Friends In Low Places • Love Can Build A Bridge • No One Else On Earth • and more.
00243165 . . . .$7.95

AS TIME GOES BY
Arranged by Joe Raposo
15 songs, including: As Time Goes By • Embraceable You • How Long Has This Been Going On • Misty • The More I See You • Someone To Watch Over Me and more.
00001021 . . . .$7.95

FAVORITE STANDARDS FROM YESTERYEAR
18 songs, including: Blue Moon • Isn't It Romantic • Love Is A Many Splendored Thing • Mona Lisa • Moon River • Over The Rainbow and more.
00001615 . . . .$7.95

FROM A DISTANCE (AND OTHER EASY LISTENING FAVORITES)
14 favorites, including: After The Lovin' • Love Story (Where Do I Begin?) • We've Only Just Begun • You Light Up My Life • and more.
00001616 . . . .$7.95

GREAT MOVIE SONGS OF ALL TIME
16 songs, including Arthur's Theme (Best That You Can Do) • Chariots Of Fire • (Everything I Do) I Do It For You • Theme From Ice Castles (Through The Eyes Of Love) • Up Where We Belong • and more.
00001614 . . . .$7.95

FOR MORE INFORMATION, SEE YOUR LOCAL MUSIC DEALER, OR WRITE TO:

HAL•LEONARD CORPORATION

7777 W. BLUEMOUND RD. P.O. BOX 13819 MILWAUKEE, WI 53213

Prices, availability, and contents subject to change without notice.
Some products may not be available outside the U.S.A.

CHRISTMAS AT THE PIANO
30 songs: Have Yourself A Merry Little Christmas • I'll Be Home For Christmas • Let It Snow! Let It Snow! Let It Snow! • Silver Bells • and more holiday favorites.
00001491 . . . .$7.95

FRIENDS AND LOVERS
Arranged by Joe Raposo
14 songs, featuring: Both To Each Other • Evergreen • Killing Me Softly With His Song • Saving All My Love For You • We've Got Tonight • You've Lost That Loving Feeling and more.
00001023 . . . .$7.95

BROADWAY FAVORITES
20 favorite songs, including: Climb Ev'ry Mountain • Getting To Know You • I Dreamed A Dream • Let Me Entertain You • Memory • and more.
00243162 . . .$8.95

JAZZ CLASSICS
20 songs, including: April In Paris • Don't Get Around Much Anymore • How High The Moon • It Don't Mean A Thing (If It Ain't Got That Swing) • When I Fall In Love • and more.
00243163 . . . .$7.95

THE PHANTOM OF THE OPERA
9 songs from the Broadway smash, including: All I Ask Of You • Angel Of Music • The Phantom Of The Opera • The Music Of The Night • and more.
00001632 . . . .$12.95